THE MYSTERIOUS MAYA CIVILIZATION

By Emily Mahoney

Portions of this book originally appeared in *Maya Civilization* by Charles and Linda George.

LUCENT
P R E S S

Published in 2018 by
Lucent Press, an Imprint of Greenhaven Publishing, LLC
353 3rd Avenue
Suite 255
New York, NY 10010

Designer: Seth Hughes
Editor: Nicole Horning

Library of Congress Cataloging-in-Publication Data

Names: Mahoney, Emily Jankowski, author.
Title: The mysterious Maya civilization / Emily Mahoney.
Description: New York : Lucent Press, 2018. | Series: World history |
   Includes bibliographical references and index.
Identifiers: LCCN 2017038641 | ISBN 9781534561861 (library bound book) ISBN: 9781534563094
   (paperback)
Subjects: LCSH: Mayas–Juvenile literature. | Mayas–Social life and
   customs–Juvenile literature. | Civilization, Ancient–Juvenile literature.
Classification: LCC F1435 .M353 2018 | DDC 972.81/016–dc23
LC record available at https://lccn.loc.gov/2017038641

CPSIA compliance information: Batch #CW18KL: For further information contact Greenhaven Publishing LLC, New York, New York at 1-844-317-7404.

Please visit our website, www.greenhavenpublishing.com. For a free color catalog of all our
high-quality books, call toll free 1-844-317-7404 or fax 1-844-317-7405.

Contents

Foreword

History books are often filled with names and dates—words and numbers for students to memorize for a test and forget once they move on to another class. However, what history books should be filled with are great stories, because the history of our world is filled with great stories. Love, death, violence, heroism, and betrayal are not just themes found in novels and movie scripts. They are often the driving forces behind major historical events.

When told in a compelling way, fact is often far more interesting—and sometimes far more unbelievable—than fiction. World history is filled with more drama than the best television shows, and all of it really happened. As readers discover the incredible truth behind the triumphs and tragedies that have impacted the world since ancient times, they also come to understand that everything is connected. Historical events do not exist in a vacuum. The stories that shaped world history continue to shape the present and will undoubtedly shape the future.

The titles in this series aim to provide readers with a comprehensive understanding of pivotal events in world history. They are written with a focus on providing readers with multiple perspectives to help them develop an appreciation for the complexity of the study of history. There is no set lens through which history must be viewed, and these titles encourage readers to analyze different viewpoints to understand why a historical figure acted the way they did or why a contemporary scholar wrote what they did about a historical event. In this way, readers are able to sharpen their critical-thinking skills and apply those skills in their history classes. Readers are aided in this pursuit by formally documented quotations and annotated bibliographies, which encourage further research and debate.

Many of these quotations come from carefully selected primary sources, including diaries, public records, and contemporary research and writings. These valuable primary sources helps readers hear the voices of those who directly experienced historical events, as well as the voices of biographers and historians who provide a unique perspective on familiar topics. Their voices all help history come alive in a vibrant way.

As students read the titles in this series, they are provided with clear context in the form of maps, timelines, and informative text. These elements give them the basic facts they need to fully appreciate the high drama that is history.

The study of history is difficult at times—not because of all the information that needs to be memorized, but because of the challenging questions it asks us. How could something as horrible as the Holocaust happen? Why would religious leaders use torture during the Inquisition? Why does ISIS have so many followers? The information presented in each title gives readers the tools they need to confront these questions and participate in the debates they inspire.

As we pore over the stories of events and eras that changed the world, we come to understand a simple truth: No one can escape being a part of history. We are not bystanders; we are active participants in the stories that are being created now and will be written about in history books decades and even centuries from now. The titles in this series help readers gain a deeper appreciation for history and a stronger understanding of the connection between the stories of the past and the stories they are part of right now.

SETTING THE SCENE: A TIMELINE

3000 BC ·········· 1800 BC–AD 250 ·········· AD 250–900 ·········· 378 ·········· 600 ··········

The Maya civilization's Classic Period—Maya cities flourish during this time.

The Preclassic Period of the Maya civilization occurs; agriculture is effective and widespread; some of the largest pyramids are built during this time.

A volcanic eruption buries the Maya city of Cerén in modern-day El Salvador.

The earliest form of writing, cuneiform, is introduced in Sumer.

Fire is Born (Siyaj K'ak'), a warlord from Teotihuacan in central Mexico, invades Tikal.

The story of Spanish soldier and excavator Antonio del Río is published, which inspires further expeditions; John Lloyd Stephens and Frederick Catherwood travel to the Yucatán and Guatemala; Stephens's *Incidents of Travel in Central America, Chiapas, and Yucatán* is published.

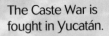
The Caste War is fought in Yucatán.

Rigoberta Menchú Tum, a Guatemalan Maya, is awarded the Nobel Peace Prize.

The last date recorded on a stela in the Maya city of Tonina.

The last dated monument is erected in Tikal, signaling the city's collapse.

MAYA CIVILIZATION: UNRAVELING THE MYSTERY

The Maya people have been called many names over the years, such as "the mysterious Maya" and "the magnificent Maya," and many scholarly books and articles have been written about this ancient Mesoamerican civilization. Today, much of the mystery surrounding this group of people from Southern Mexico and Central America is being revealed, and anthropologists are learning that the culture of the Maya is no longer lost.

Many years before European explorers came to the New World, the Maya people were building huge cities, studying astrology, and creating a complex written language in the jungles and coastal plains of Mesoamerica—a cultural region including both Mexico and parts of Central America. Spanish conquerors did not arrive until the 1500s, but by that time, the Maya cities were already abandoned and in a state of ruin.

Despite the fact that the classic Maya civilization is no longer in existence, the Maya culture is still thriving. Today, more than 6 million Maya people live in Mexican states such as Yucatán, Quintana Roo, and Chiapas, as well as in the Central American nations of Belize, Guatemala, and the western portions of Honduras and El Salvador. They are the largest group of indigenous peoples north of Peru.

Most people, however, still think of the people who lived centuries ago when they hear the term "Maya," probably because they are familiar with their advanced ancient civilization. Artifacts and evidence of this advanced culture—pottery, an accurate calendar, and a complex system of hieroglyphic writing—have been unearthed in ancient cities and have been compared to the classic civilizations of Egypt, Greece, and Rome. While these people are called the Maya, it is not known for sure what they called themselves. They speak dozens of variations, or dialects, of the Mayan language, such as K'iche' and Yucatec, and still have vibrant and fascinating traditions. Scholars use the term *Mayan* to describe only the language, and for all other references to the culture, the people, or their achievements, they use *Maya*.

The Story of a Civilization

What happened to the Maya? How did they build such a vast empire only to have it crumble into ruins? Archaeologists look for answers to these questions wherever they can. For more than a century, scholars dug through ruined Maya cities looking for bits of pottery, burial sites, murals depicting everyday activities, and remnants of tools. Maya hieroglyphs were intriguing, but no one knew how to decode them. No matter how many artifacts scientists uncovered, they were never enough to paint a complete picture of the Maya.

Archaeological evidence tells only part of the story. Written records yield much more specific information, such as names, dates, and major events. The Maya carved many such written records onto their buildings and monuments. They also created thousands of codices—books made from rectangular pieces of bark covered with a type of plaster, tied together, and folded accordion style. Unfortunately, much of what Maya scribes wrote in

those books no longer exists. The vast majority of the codices were destroyed at the time of the Spanish conquest by priests who believed those books and the strange markings and symbols they contained were the work of the devil. The primary architect of that destruction was Diego de Landa, who, on July 12, 1562, ordered the burning of 5,000 Maya idols and dozens of codices.

Today, due to recent breakthroughs in decoding Maya hieroglyphs, archaeologists are finding answers to questions that have interested them for decades. They are learning, for example, that influence from Teotihuacan, the sprawling city of more than 100,000 people in the valley of Mexico, helped spur the blossoming of Maya culture during the Classic Period.

Even though there is still much that historians do not know about the Maya people, scholars have developed several theories of what caused their downfall. First, many believe that the Maya had depleted their resources from the areas around them to the point where they could not sustain themselves in the area any longer. Other scholars argue that warfare caused a collapse in trade, their military, and their dynastic power, resulting in chaos. Lastly, scholars also theorize that a catastrophic change in the environment, such as a drought, wiped out their civilization.

While there is not an agreement on what exactly caused the collapse of the Maya civilization, archaeologists are not giving up on finding solid information to answer that question. There are still archaeological digs happening at many Maya sites, and new technology is even being used at previously excavated, or dug up, sites to see what else

Scientists are piecing together artifacts, remains, and architecture, such as this temple in the city of Tulum, to try to figure out what happened to the Maya and how they lived.

can be learned. Some of these studies include radiocarbon dating, which was used in a study published in 2017 that revealed new clues about political instability and warfare contributing to the collapse of the Maya.

CHAPTER ONE

THE MAYA RISE TO POWER

T he Maya civilization continues to intrigue scholars and average people. The interest in this ancient civilization stems partly from the fact that there is so much mystery surrounding their culture. Who were these ancient people, and how were they able to create such an advanced system of living? What was their daily life like, and how did their civilization fall? Answers to questions such as these can be found by closely examining Maya sites and artifacts, and by doing this, archaeologists are piecing together some of the details of their fascinating lives.

Breakthroughs in Understanding the Maya

No area of archaeological study has undergone a more radical change during the past few decades than the study of the ancient Maya civilization. Major scientific investigations—primarily delving into how climate change may have affected the course of Maya history—are shedding light on unanswered questions scientists and scholars have been posing for more than a century about the origin, history, lifestyle, and decline of the Maya.

Breakthroughs in the decoding of Maya hieroglyphs are revealing the names of the kings and queens of individual city-states as well as dates and records of their political activities, alliances, achievements, wars, and rituals. The hieroglyphs also show the large influence of other advanced civilizations on the Maya's development.

Since the 1960s, evidence has emerged that has helped scholars gain a more thorough understanding of who the Maya actually were. According to Nikolai Grube, a professor of Maya studies in Germany,

There are scarcely any other areas of archaeology where interpretations and ideas have changed so completely

as in the field of Maya studies ... Although up to just a few decades ago it was still believed that the Maya had been peace-loving maize farmers who obeyed their priests' exhortations to observe the stars and honor time, it has now been proven that they were ruled over by kings and princes who were just as power-hungry and vain as [rulers] elsewhere in the world ... The extensive Preclassic cities in northern Guatemala were unknown until just a few years ago. New excavations there have caused us to date the beginning of urban civilization back by about half a millennium.[1]

Discoveries of ruins, such as these from the ancient Maya city of Uxmal, help people to learn more about the Maya and their way of life.

A COMPLICATED EXPEDITION

John Lloyd Stephens, an American archaeologist, was sent to Central America for diplomatic business for U.S. president Martin Van Buren. He departed for Honduras on October 3, 1839, accompanied by Frederick Catherwood. Once his diplomatic duties were completed, Stephens and Catherwood explored the Maya ruins of Copán and eventually ended up at Palenque.

They traveled hundreds of miles over trails bordered by volcanoes, through thick jungles, and over steep mountain ranges. They crossed rivers using dangerous bridges made of tree trunks lashed together or braided lianas (vines). They slept in the ruins. While Stephens recorded their adventures, Catherwood created beautifully detailed images of what he saw using a camera lucida. A camera lucida used a prism to project the image of an object onto a piece of drawing paper. Catherwood later colored his lithographs with pastels.

This is one of Catherwood's drawings of a traditional Maya structure. Drawings such as this were included in Stephens's book about their travels.

Early Explorers

Spanish priests and travelers during the 16th, 17th, and 18th centuries marveled at the ruins of gigantic pyramids they saw in Yucatán cities such as Uxmal, Tulum, Palenque, and Chichén Itzá. They wondered who had designed and constructed these amazing structures. Some early visitors theorized that one of the lost groups of Israel may have settled there. Others felt it must have been ancestors of some European or Asian culture—perhaps the Welsh, Vikings, Phoenicians, or Tartars.

Not until the 1800s did interest in Maya ruins begin to grow and be associated with the Maya themselves. In 1822, a London firm published the story of a Spanish soldier, Antonio del Río, who had visited and excavated in the Maya city of Palenque during the late 18th century. His detailed account encouraged further expeditions. In 1839, American archaeologist and traveler John Lloyd Stephens and British artist and architect Frederick Catherwood traveled to the Yucatán and then to Guatemala. They visited various sites—some on the scrub plains of Yucatán and some deep in Central American jungles—and recorded their experiences in journals. Accompanying their dramatic written accounts were intricate line drawings that depicted what they had seen.

With the publication of Stephens's *Incidents of Travel in Central America, Chiapas, and Yucatán* in 1841, interest in the Maya spread. However, due to the remoteness of most of the ruins and their overgrown conditions—as well as the heat, insects, and snakes of the tropics—only a handful of individuals and organizations were willing to devote themselves to Maya study.

Another reason that the Maya fascinated people during the mid-1800s was the perception among most Europeans and Americans that such civilizations were beyond the capabilities of Mesoamerican cultures. In his 1948 book about Stephens, late historian Victor Wolfgang von Hagen explained this attitude:

The acceptance of an "Indian civilization" demanded, to an American living in 1839, an entire reorientation, for to him an Indian was one of those barbaric [people] against whom wars were constantly waged ... Nor did one ever think of calling the other indigenous inhabitants of the continent "civilized." In the universally accepted opinion, they were like their North American counterparts—savages. No one dreamed that throughout the tablelands of Mexico, in the tangled, scrub-jungles of Yucatán, there stood, covered by jungle [vegetation], ruins of temples, acropolises, and stone causeways of a civilization as great in extent as Egypt's ... "Aztec," "Maya," "Toltec," and "Inca" were in no dictionary, and in few histories. These civilizations were not only dead, for dead implied having once lived, but, even to the world immersed in searching out the antique, absolutely unknown.[2]

THE FASCINATING STUDY OF THE MAYA

Maya culture continues to be a fascinating subject for scholars. Nikolai Grube, a professor of Maya studies, explained what is so compelling about Maya culture in the book *Maya: Divine Kings of the Rain Forest*:

> *Where else in the world are complete sites of an ancient culture hidden deep in the jungle; where else are complete regions just blank areas on the archaeological map? Where else do we know so little about the economic foundations of an ancient civilization? And where else in the world have all the great cities of a culture sunk without a trace, abandoned by their inhabitants for no apparent reason? ...*
>
> *We now have a picture of the rise and development of Maya culture that makes former representations look like rough sketches. Whereas the focus of older works focused on the exoticism of the Maya, on their differentness and uniqueness, modern publications ... show the Maya to have been people whose problems, intentions, and motives were not so different from those of other people all over the world.[1]*

1. Nikolai Grube, ed., *Maya: Divine Kings of the Rain Forest*. Nordrhein-Westfalen, DE: h.f.ullmann, 2007, pp. 12–13.

Despite this misguided belief that these cultures were somehow beneath the Europeans, governments, museums, and individuals saw the opportunity to gain fame by studying these ruins and bringing artifacts back for their national museums. An Englishman, Alfred Percival Maudslay, following in the footsteps of Stephens and Catherwood, arrived in Guatemala in 1881 to begin what would become a 20-year study of Maya ruins.

Setting the Bar High

Maudslay pioneered archaeological methods that have been used for more than a century—clearing vegetation to reveal structures, measuring and drawing maps of cities, making plaster casts of carvings to be studied later, and photographing hieroglyphs to better enable their analysis. His trek began at the Maya "lost cities" of Quiriguá, located in eastern Guatemala, and Copán, located to the south in far western

Maudslay, shown here, not only cleared much of the brush surrounding the pyramids he found, but he also created beautiful dry-plate photographs that showed his experiences.

Honduras. He eventually extended his study to Tikal, becoming the second foreigner to reach that remote northern Guatemalan site.

Maudslay recorded his experiences with dry-plate photographs and in scientific notebooks. In his writings, however, he chose to focus not on the exciting sense of discovery he must have felt but rather on the hard work he saw before him. Maudslay wrote upon arriving at Quiriguá,

> Overhead and all around was a dense tropical forest; the undergrowth was so dense that we had difficulty in finding any of the monuments and even when within touch of them, so thickly were they covered with creepers, ferns and moss that it was not easy to distinguish them from dead tree trunks. However, we pulled off the creepers and then scrubbed away the moss with some rough brushes we made out of the midribs of the palm leaflets and, as the sculptures began to show up, I sacrificed one of my ivory-backed hair brushes out of my dressing bag to clear out the more delicate carving of the hieroglyphics.[3]

He later wrote of the unexpected beauty of the structures of Copán; yet upon arriving at Tikal on Easter Sunday 1881, Maudslay again focused his written account on how completely overgrown the ruins appeared: "On the whole I must own to being much disappointed. The forest was over everything. The work of clearing would be much more than I could do and there appeared to be very little hope of taking satisfactory photographs."[4]

Maudslay and his porters eventually cleared much of the brush covering the central pyramids of Tikal. His photographs, published between 1889 and 1902 in *Biología Centrali-Americana*, a five-volume work about his discoveries in Guatemala, provided a first look to the world at these magnificent structures. His clear photographs revealed details that Catherwood's pen-and-ink sketches could not. Scholars who were unable to make the difficult journey to Central America could now study Maudslay's photographs and learn more about Maya hieroglyphs.

The Earliest Maya People

Maudslay's work inspired scholars and universities to begin their own excavations. Large-scale excavations and restorations, mostly funded by American universities, were on a much grander scale than those done previously. The Peabody Museum of Harvard, the University of Pennsylvania, the Carnegie Institute of Washington, Tulane University, and the Institute of Anthropology and History in Mexico each sent teams of archaeologists. Many of their projects continued well into the 20th century, greatly adding to the world's knowledge of the Maya.

Scholars have divided the chronology of Mesoamerican civilizations into specific periods of time, depending on levels of technology, architecture, and social structure. These classifications—Paleo-Indian, Archaic, Preclassic, Classic, and Postclassic—are further divided into sub-categories. As new discoveries are made, however, scientists sometimes have to rethink their table of organization.

Evidence of humans—spear points, obsidian blades, and residue of camp-fires—has been dated to around 10,500 BC in caves in the highlands of Guatemala, specifically at a site called Los Tapiales. These early inhabitants lived during what scientists call the Paleo-Indian Period, extending from 14,000 years ago to around 8000 BC.

During the following era—the Archaic Period, which lasted from around 8000 to 2000 BC—groups of hunter-gatherers gradually settled in small villages. Each village probably consisted of members of an extended family and were led by the patriarch—the eldest male. These early villagers began growing wild plants to add to their food supply, thus beginning the practice of agriculture. They also arranged their villages in a particular pattern that continues in use today.

The *Plazuela*

A culture arranges its homesteads, villages, and cities in what is called a settlement pattern. The basic settlement pattern of the Maya was the *plazuela*, or "plaza group." It originated during the Archaic Period and developed grad-ually throughout the various stages of Maya history. In a *plazuela*, several

houses are typically placed facing each other, with a communal area in the center. This arrangement was evident in all levels of Maya society—from the Archaic Period to modern times, and from the simplest farm home to the largest city.

Arthur Demarest, a professor of an-thropology at Vanderbilt University, described how the Maya eventually ex-panded the basic *plazuela* arrangement into larger communities:

> *Usually, several houses of closely related families are placed facing each other around open courtyard living areas. In turn, several of these "plaza groups" are often placed together to form tiny*

Temples, palaces, and other settlements in ancient Maya cities often surrounded a central plaza. The temple shown here borders a central plaza in the plazuela *pattern that developed throughout Maya history.*

hamlets of related extended families ...

In the ancient Maya lowland sites in pre-Columbian times, such ... associated structures often were placed in somewhat more regular rectangular arrangements of two, three, or four platforms with huts facing each other around an open courtyard or plaza. The latter served as a living and work area for the family, as did platforms or level areas behind and near the plaza group.[5]

The same basic pattern is found in the ruins of Maya cities—with temples, palaces, and ball courts surrounding a central plaza.

A shared kitchen garden, still a common feature in rural Mexico and Guatemala, lay outside homes and other outbuildings in a typical rural *plazuela*. Chemical analysis of soil around ancient house mounds—raised earthen platforms left behind when huts that stood on them decayed—verifies that the areas had been under cultivation. As in modern times, these kitchen gardens were used for growing plants such as squash, beans, and chili peppers to be eaten or sold at market as well as herbs for seasoning and for medicinal purposes.

The Formative Period

The Archaic Period was followed by the Preclassic Period, which extended from 1800 BC to AD 250. Some scholars call this the Formative Period because it includes the centuries during which the Maya first began to exhibit cultural characteristics that were different from other groups. These include the rise of city-states, which were individual cities that were ruled by a king or queen. These rulers' power extended to the countryside and villages immediately surrounding the city. Unlike the Aztecs of central Mexico and the Incas of South America, the Maya never unified into a single empire. Instead they evolved into a less centralized feudal society. During the Preclassic period, the Maya also developed large-scale ceremonial architecture and the beginnings of hieroglyphics. The Preclassic Period is further divided into the Early Preclassic Period (1800 to 1000 BC), the Middle Preclassic Period (1000 to 300 BC), and the Late Preclassic Period (300 BC to AD 250).

The Maya of the Early Preclassic Period

The Maya of the Early Preclassic Period exhibited many distinct characteristics. Larger multifamily villages, led by a chief, were established. Agriculture was expanded to include more crops and improved farming techniques.

More sophisticated art was evident in the manufacture and use of ceramics and in the development of iconographic artistic expression—the painting and carving of images of people and symbols representing ideas or events. The Maya of the Early Preclassic Period also exhibited the beginnings of a more complex, hierarchical society. During this era, cultures across Mesoamerica first developed the basics of writing systems and an interest in measuring time and in studying astronomy and space.

Evidence uncovered at Cuello, an Early Preclassic site in northern Belize, indicates that these early Maya all lived in pole-and-thatch huts constructed on low dirt platforms. Archaeologists have discovered clusters of these platforms, along with artifacts left behind by the people who lived there. Evidence also shows the expanded cultivation of crops such as maize, beans, squash, and manioc.

The manufacture of ceramics is further evidence that the early Maya were settling into more permanent home bases. Particular examples of this art form have been found at Cuello as well as along Guatemala's Pacific Coast lowlands at Monte Alto, La Blanca, Ocós, El Mesak, and Ujuxte. At some Early Preclassic sites along the Pacific Coast of the Mexican state of Chiapas—at sites such as Izapa and Ojo de Agua—ceramics and stone carvings have a resemblance to art from the Olmec culture that developed about the same time

THE OLMEC CULTURE

The Olmec culture developed in the forested lowlands of the Gulf Coast region of southeastern Mexico, southeast of present-day Veracruz. It thrived from 1200 to 400 BC and was long thought to have been the *cultura madre*, or "mother culture," of Mesoamerica. The Olmec people were thought to have created the first cities, the first monumental structures, and a remarkably accurate calendar; they also developed a particular type of ball game that became a common feature of many Mesoamerican cultures. Discoveries along the Pacific Coast of southern Mexico and Guatemala, however, have been tentatively classified as early Maya and may prove to have been built as early as, or perhaps before, anything built by the Olmec.

on the southern Gulf Coast of Mexico. These similarities indicate that the two cultures must have made contact.

A Class Structure Develops

During the Middle Preclassic Period, from 1000 to 300 BC, a more hierarchical class structure continued to develop. The old tribal society became more similar to the feudal society of medieval Europe or the city-states of ancient Greece, with leadership in the hands of a single king or queen and an elite upper class to support that ruler. Members of the developing Maya upper class were either religious, military, or political leaders. Such leaders generally demanded the construction of public structures. Many of these structures were used for governmental or religious ceremonies, but others were monuments and ornate tombs

to honor the leaders themselves. Examples of such public architecture can be seen in the Pacific Coast lowlands of Guatemala at Tak'alik Ab'aj and at Kaminaljuyú in that nation's central highlands.

During the final centuries of the Middle Preclassic Period, the Maya spread farther inland from the Pacific Coast areas. During these years, they established ceremonial centers at Piedras Negras, Seibal, Cival, Dos Pilas, and El Perú, expanding steadily toward the north and east. They carried with them the trend toward larger ceremonial centers and more extensive public architecture.

Archaeologists have discovered two of the largest ceremonial centers ever built by the Maya at Nakbe and El Mirador in the Petén region of northern Guatemala. El Mirador, for example, features two of the largest Maya pyramids—La Danta and El Tigre—which compare in size with the Great Pyramid in Egypt. Archaeologists believe these structures were used as raised platforms for religious ceremonies. No tombs have been discovered beneath them.

Further Developments

In the Late Preclassic Period, from 300 BC to about AD 250, the Maya further developed their writing system, their calendar, their interest in astronomy, and their level of artistic expression. These intellectual developments are demonstrated in temples with stuccoed and painted facades (the front of a building), such as those found at El Mirador, and in dramatic murals, such as those discovered at San Bartolo in northeastern Guatemala.

The Late Preclassic is the period of Maya history that has undergone the most rethinking due to discoveries in the jungles of northern Guatemala and the coastal regions of Guatemala and El Salvador. These discoveries have proven that the Maya civilization of the Late Preclassic Period already displayed characteristics, beliefs, and practices that formerly were only associated with the Classic Period.

The Maya Golden Age

The Maya enjoyed their golden age from AD 250 to 900, which is also known as the Classic Period. Many city-states changed from simply ceremonial centers into full cities, some with populations in the tens of thousands. Each city was ruled by a succession of kings or queens, who got support from their nobility. These noblemen oversaw the day-to-day operations of the city-state. Some of the kings from the city-states during the Classic Period may have been outsiders—nobles from Teotihuacan, for example. During the Classic Period, the Maya civilization reached its peak of population and the top of its intellectual achievement, yet it never came together into a centralized empire.

Each Maya city-state featured a huge, beautifully decorated ceremonial center with steep-sided pyramids topped with temples and palaces. These pyramids were constantly being rebuilt, layer upon layer. Beyond the ceremonial center were outlying structures that housed artisans, craftsmen, and bureaucrats. Farther out, and in the surrounding countryside, were farmers and laborers who supported the elite. Most of these city-states were located in the Petén region of northern Guatemala and in the southern Yucatán lowlands.

Many of the characteristics that originated during earlier periods of Maya history were passed down to the Classic Period, such as a fascination with astronomy, the recording of the passage of time in a calendar, artistic expression, a system of writing, and the construction of public monuments. All of these were recorded on the stone stela, an architectural feature that set apart the Maya cities that were built during this

Shown here is one example of a Maya stela created during the Classic Period.

period. A stela is a stone column built in a public location to honor a particular event or person—generally the birth, marriage, rise to the throne, military victory, or death of a king or queen.

Classic Maya cities have many stelae, whereas cities constructed earlier—during the Preclassic Period—do not. These stelae are one of the few remaining written records of Classic Maya history, since so many of their books, or codices, were lost to fires started by Spanish priests. Additionally, many stelae have been worn down over time, making those that have survived even more valuable.

Each stela has the face of a mythological creature or actual ruler on one side, with carvings of dates, names, and events on the other. People were able to view them in central areas, such as in front of temples and palaces. As of 2017, the earliest dated stela sits in the central plaza of Tikal, with the equivalent of the date AD 292 carved onto its side. The latest stands at Tonina, in southern Mexico, and is dated AD 909.

The stelae of the Classic Maya cities have revealed specific information about those cities and the leaders who ruled them. They provide clues about the relations between individual Maya city-states, including their alliances and wars. The stelae have also helped fill gaps in scholars' understanding of Maya society during the Classic Period.

One particular stela—Stela 31 in Tikal—has now been decoded and proves a long-held theory. The stela provides written evidence that an invasion by an outside force significantly changed the development of Classic Maya civilization.

"Fire is Born"

According to the hieroglyphic record of Stela 31, the invasion occurred on January 8, 378. A large, well-armed force from the mighty city of Teotihuacan in central Mexico arrived at the Maya city of Waka (now called El Perú) in present-day northern Guatemala.

Teotihuacan, shown here, was a great city that is known for having the third-largest pyramid in the world, the Pyramid of the Sun.

At the head of this invading army was a warlord named Siyaj K'ak'—"Fire is Born." Dressed in extravagant feathered headdresses and carrying weapons and mirrored shields, Fire is Born's army impressed the local ruler, Sun-faced Jaguar. Sun-faced Jaguar welcomed the envoy into his city and formed an alliance between his city and Teotihuacan.

Fire is Born's ultimate goal, according to Stela 31, was the conquest of Tikal, a major Maya city-state some 50 miles (80 km) to the east. His mission, it seems, was to bring the region of north-central Guatemala under Teotihuacan's control. To do this, he recruited additional warriors from Waka and marched on to Tikal less than a week later. After defeating that city's army on January 16, his forces killed Tikal's king, Chak Tok Ich'aak—Jaguar Paw—and destroyed most of that city's stone stelae, replacing them with their own, celebrating their victory. According to Stela 31, which was built a generation later, Fire is Born was proclaimed "Lord of the West" and later ruled over a new foreign ruler, perhaps a son of the ruler of Teotihuacan, Spear-thrower Owl.

Until the arrival of Fire is Born, the Maya remained politically fragmented, each city-state charting its own path. After AD 378, Maya culture blossomed, alliances were formed between city-states, and great advances in science and technology took place. According to author Guy Gugliotta in an article for *National Geographic*,

> *Though fragmentary, the evidence that has emerged over the past decade suggests that this mysterious outsider remade the political leadership of the Maya world. Mixing diplomacy and force, he forged alliances, installed new dynasties, and spread the influence of the distant city-state he represented, the great metropolis of Teotihuacan near present-day Mexico City.*[6]

Over the following decades, Fire is Born's name appeared on monuments all across the Maya's territory. In his wake, the Maya of the Classic Period achieved a level of civilization unsurpassed in the Americas that endured for more than 500 years.

CHapTer TWO

NOBLE MAYA PEOPLE

The Maya people had an organized class system that was very strict, and many scholars believe this helped their society to function in such an advanced way. From noble upper class members to poor farmers and commoners, each person had a role to play that helped their city-state to thrive. Evidence from Maya tombs help to show how these people looked and acted. The nobility of the Classic Period were particularly stylish and wanted to show their wealth off to other people in their community.

Maya Society

The Classic Period of Maya history ended centuries before the arrival of the Spanish. Therefore, most of what scholars know today about the upper classes of Maya society comes from archaeological evidence found in their cities. This evidence includes the tombs of Maya kings, the carved records of the stelae, and detailed images and hieroglyphs on ceramic vessels and murals. In the ruins of the Maya city of Bonampak, located in the western edge of the Mexican state of Chiapas, ornate murals inside the tomb of a Maya king paint a vivid picture of life at court during the Classic Period. These include detailed images of how the nobility of Classic Maya city-states looked—what physical features and accessories they considered stylish.

In these images, Maya society is portrayed as having strict social classes, with a king and queen at the top; priests, nobles, warriors, and artisans slightly lower in rank; and common people below that. Some Maya kings ruled over only the city-state in which they lived. Others, through alliances, outside influence, intermarriages, and conquest, created dynasties that controlled several city-states from a central location.

Maya society had two classes of people: the elite and the commoners. The elite were called *ah mehenob*, or "higher men," in Yucatec, a Mayan language in

The vivid murals at Bonampak, shown here, depict much of Maya life at the time of the Classic Period, including accessories and traditions.

use at the time of the Spanish conquest that is still spoken in the region. Commoners were called *yalba uinicob*, or "lower men." The *ah mehenob* were further divided into subclasses. The ruling class—kings and queens—though few in number, occupied the highest level of society. According to hieroglyphs, the highest rank in Maya society was the *ahau*, or "lord" (sometimes spelled *ajaw*). This title was used by the ruler and others within the nobility. Beginning in the fourth century AD, however, Maya rulers referred to themselves as *k'uhal ahau*, or "divine lord." Some rulers also included the term *kaloomte* in their titles, which was a term for a supreme king or queen.

Life as a Royal Maya

The king and queen of a Maya city-state were worshipped as gods. As such, they were not expected to work like common people. They spent their time ruling over elite councils, making decisions that affected their city-state. They lived in lavish, over-the-top palaces within the city-state's ceremonial center, attended by numerous servants. According to murals found in many Classic Maya cities, each king wore a feathered headdress, a cape made from the brilliantly colored feathers of quetzal birds, intricate jade and shell jewelry, and sometimes an elaborate mask to make him appear godlike.

Much is known about Maya kings and queens because hundreds of carved stelae commemorate their achievements and still stand in the central plazas of Classic Maya ceremonial centers. The Maya called these stone monuments *lakamtuun*, or "banner stones," and built them whenever anything happened of historical note. In the book, *Chronicle of the Maya Kings and Queens*, Simon Martin and Nikolai Grube described what was generally carved on stelae: "Carved with the king's image, often shown standing on a bound captive or iconic location, their inscriptions go on to chronicle the major historical events that have occurred since the last stone was set up."[7]

Scholars often can read the stelae, murals, and pottery and know when members of the nobility were born, who their parents were, where they came from, whom they married, what they achieved during their lifetimes, and how and where they were buried. Most kings and queens were buried in elaborate tombs that featured colorful murals depicting their lives. Because much of Maya hieroglyphic writing has been translated, these individuals now have names and life stories.

Royal succession was primarily patrilineal, meaning it followed the ancestral line on the father's side. As is often the case in kingdoms, eldest sons generally became heirs to their father's throne. Princes were called *ch'ok*, meaning "young lord," and the heir apparent was called *baah ch'ok*, the "head youth." Queens did rule some Maya city-states of the Classic Period, but only when no male heir could become king and the dynasty might otherwise have fallen.

Power was passed down from generation to generation in the Maya civilization. Shown here is a tablet depicting a crown being passed from mother to son.

Ceremonies and Rituals

Scholars know that Maya kings and queens, once in power, had their lives virtually run by the rituals demanded by the complex Maya calendar. Their primary duty was to conduct public religious ceremonies—either alone or serving alongside priests—as mediators between their people and the gods. During those ceremonies, they performed ritual dances or participated in a particular ball game. They also sought visions—messages from the heavens.

Archaeologists believe the Mesoamerican ball game may have originated as early as the fifth century BC and that its popularity spread as far as the modern-day southwestern United States. Stone ball courts are present in virtually every Maya city. Most courts are I-shaped, with a long, narrow playing field surrounded by sloped or vertical walls, often with stone rings placed high on the opposing walls. The game, played in some ways like soccer, was a key element of the Maya creation story. Maya kings regularly played the game to reenact the adventures of the mythical figures called the Hero Twins, whose actions were believed to be essential to pave the way for the creation of humanity as well as to establish the relationship between the gods and humans.

Part of that relationship was communicating with their gods, and only rulers were considered worthy to receive such messages. To induce trances they believed were necessary to receive these visions, Maya kings and queens put themselves through ordeals of pain and deprivation—going without food or sleep, smoking tobacco, and inflicting wounds on themselves to allow their blood to flow. Blood, the essence of life, was sacred to the Maya, and royal blood was considered the ultimate offering to the gods. In addition to providing a blood sacrifice, the blood loss weakened the individual and helped induce the trance-like state necessary for a vision quest.

During public ceremonies, Maya kings drained blood using stingray spines, bone needles, or obsidian spikes. During these sacrifices, royal blood dripped onto fabric or paper strips, which then were burned. It was believed that smoke from the bloody paper mingled with smoke from incense burners and rose to feed the gods.

The Priesthood

Some archaeologists believe religious ceremonies were performed only by Maya kings and queens. Others, however, believe that a group of specially trained people—priests—must have performed those duties. No archaeological evidence proves conclusively that a separate class of nobles existed that served as priests during the Classic Period. However, some believe there must have been a separate class of priests because a powerful Maya priesthood existed at the time of the Spanish conquest. These scholars insist it is logical to assume that such a specialty also existed earlier in Maya history.

At the time of the conquest, the high priest in each city-state, the *Ahaucan May*, was the keeper of the calendar and the sacred chronicles—records of Maya history and astrological charts. The priest's knowledge of astronomy and mathematics allowed him to predict events such as the arrival of comets and eclipses of the sun or moon. They were also responsible for teaching and passing on the history of their people, including knowledge of Maya hieroglyphic writing.

Below the high priests were assistants who conducted most day-to-day tasks. The assistants kept temple fires burning, made sure incense burners stayed lit, and made daily offerings to the gods. These lower priests also were responsible for advising those who came to consult a priest about astrological matters—what day would be best for a wedding or what to name a child, for example. Priests lived in or near the temples and wore ornate robes and sometimes masks and headdresses.

The Noble Class

Beneath the upper *ahau* class were other nobles, many of whom served as government bureaucrats, trade representatives, diplomats, local administrators, or engineers—those who designed and supervised the building of temples, palaces, causeways, irrigation systems, and other public structures. The members of

A HEADDRESS FIT FOR A KING

Headdresses of Maya kings distinguished the ruler from others in the society, however, they also had a symbolic value for the Maya. According to Nikolai Grube,

Although the king's clothing differed from that of the commoners and the nobility in lavishness and the number of attributes, it was the headdress that distinguished him from all others. There were several different kinds of headdresses, but all contained the long, green-gold tail feathers of the quetzal bird … They formed the basis for masks of gods and animals and other objects of the greatest symbolic value that were intended to express that the wearer was under the protection of the gods …

Because they were believed to have a soul, the headdress and other attributes of power [of a king who had died] had to be looked after and cared for like living things; in particular, they had to be provided with nourishment in the form of offerings such as blood and incense.[1]

1. Nikolai Grube, ed., *Maya: Divine Kings of the Rain Forest*. Nordrhein-Westfalen, DE: h.f.ullmann, 2007, pp. 96–97.

The king's headdress was large and symbolic, as shown by this statue from the Yucatán.

this level of Maya nobility were wealthy landowners called *uytzam chinamital*. They shared the easy lifestyle of the king. Their homes—fine stone buildings with roofs of stone—were clustered near ceremonial centers. They, too, wore fine robes and jewelry, and many were buried in decorated tombs.

Another important member of Classic Maya nobility was the *aj tz'ib*, the scribe. Unlike the priest, who recorded historical events hieroglyphically, the scribe's role was more closely related to that of an accountant, keeping track of taxes and tributes and making sure everyone paid what they owed the king. Commoners were required to pay taxes (generally food, cloth, feathers, or other items of value), and representatives from conquered lands were required to pay tribute to the king with valuable items such as jade, obsidian, feathers, or cacao beans. Martin and Grube explained the importance of

PROVING ONE'S WORTH

In Maya society, a young heir had to go through a series of initiation rites, starting when they were five or six years old and continuing through the enthronement. In the book, *Chronicle of the Maya Kings and Queens*, Simon Martin and Nikolai Grube described how a young heir had to prove their worth:

Childhood was marked by a series of initiation rites, one of the more important being a bloodletting usually performed at the age of five or six ... Although [their lineage] was their main claim to legitimacy, [older] candidates still had to prove themselves in war. A bout of captive-taking often preceded elevation to office ...

Kingly investitures [ceremonies celebrating the crowning of a new king] were elaborate affairs made up of a series of separate acts. There was an enthronement, the heir's seating on a cushion of jaguar skin, sometimes atop an elevated scaffold bedecked with celestial symbolism and accompanied by human sacrifice. A scarf bearing a jade image of huunal, *the "Jester God" ... an ancient patron of royal authority, would be tied to his forehead. An elaborate headdress of jade and shell mosaic, trailing green iridescent plumes of the quetzal bird, would follow ... The name carried in childhood was now joined by k'uhul k'aba' "divine name," usually taken from a predecessor, sometimes a grandparent.*[1]

1. Simon Martin and Nikolai Grube, *Chronicle of the Maya Kings and Queens: Deciphering the Dynasties of the Ancient Maya*. London, UK: Thames & Hudson, 2000, p. 14.

scribes as portrayed in murals and on painted ceramics:

Tribute scenes show the king seated on a [large] throne covered with jaguar skin. Vassals kneel before him holding out bundles of fine materials, feathers and bags of cacao beans … [The aj tz'ib] compared the goods being handed over with their list of tributes. Such scenes give a rare insight into the economics of the Maya states and show that one of the king's most important activities was that of increasing his personal wealth as well as that of the society as a whole.[8]

Beauty and Appearance

Public displays of wealth and physical decorations were very important to Maya nobility because they demonstrated their social status. Hairstyles, clothing, jewelry, tattoos, and intentional scars were part of their public image. One of the most visible examples of this was how they styled their hair. Maya men generally wore headdresses with their hair long, either braided around the head with strands hanging down the back, or braided with feathers or ribbon. At times, a man might cut the hair on top of his head short or burn it off as part of the overall design. Facial hair was discouraged, and many pulled it out with copper tweezers. Women's hairstyles could be quite elaborate. They formed their hair into sculptural designs—mostly on top of their heads—and fixed it in place with tree

sap, honey, or other things that dried in place. Some women's hairstyles stood more than 1 foot (0.3 m) above their heads.

Tattooing, intentional scarring, and body paintings were common for both Maya men and women. Elite Maya would use colors and designs that showed their position in society. Tattoo designs were pricked into the skin with a sharp bone, and colored pigment was then rubbed into the wounds. This was an extremely painful experience, so tattoos represented courage and bravery. For intentional scarring, the skin would be cut or pierced in the desired pattern to create a raised scar. Then, to make sure more scars would form, the individual encouraged the growth of the scars by keeping the wounds open for a time. Any adult without tattoos and scarring patterns was looked down upon.

Michael D. Coe, a former professor of anthropology at Yale University, discussed body ornamentation in the book *The Maya*. According to Coe, the Classic Maya thought certain physical adornments enhanced their appearance or publicly identified them with a particular social class:

Both men and women had their frontal teeth filed in various patterns, and we have many ancient Maya skulls in which the incisors have been decorated with small plaques of jade. Until marriage, young men painted themselves black (and so did warriors at all times);

tattooing and decorative scarification began after wedlock, both men and women being richly elaborated from the waist up by these means.[9]

The colors used for body and face painting were very important to Maya men. Young unmarried warriors and men who were fasting painted themselves black. Blue was the color of priests, and women generally painted their faces red.

The Maya worked hard to keep their foreheads dramatically sloped, which is something unique to their culture. This, however, was not something that occurred naturally. It had to be shaped very early in life in order to form the head into what the Maya felt was a noble appearance. According to Coe,

Most Maya people had some form of body markings, such as the ones shown here. They believed that marking one's body was a display of strength.

JADE: THE MAYA'S PRECIOUS STONE

Few materials are as durable as jade. In Mesoamerica, it was prized above all other stones. Jade is green, and to the Maya, it symbolized the color of sprouting maize (corn). Maya artisans carved it into jewelry for the nobility, but commoners also decorated themselves with necklaces of small jade beads that they passed on from generation to generation.

Jade is a collective term for several types of green or blue stones, including albite, chrysopras, serpentine, and a combination of jadeite and diopside. All jade processed in Mesoamerica originated in the valley of the Rio Motagua in southern Guatemala. It was found as loose rocks and stones, ranging in size from gravel to rocks weighing several hundred pounds. Cutting jade was relatively simple. First, a sharp obsidian blade was used to score the rock. Then rope, a flat piece of hardwood, or a piece of slate was moved back and forth—with sand, crushed obsidian, or jade dust acting as an abrasive—to slowly cut halfway through the rock. The jade was then turned over, and the procedure was repeated. When only a thin section remained, a sharp blow completed the cutting.

Jade was one of the Maya's most prized materials. The material was often crafted into jewelry or masks such as those shown here.

"Immediately after birth, Yucatecan mothers washed their infants and then fastened them to a cradle, their little heads compressed between two boards in such a way that after two days a permanent fore-and-aft flattening had taken place which the Maya considered a mark of beauty."[10]

Another practice, generally done at the same time, was an attempt to cross the child's eyes. This was also considered a mark of beauty and distinction among Maya upper classes, and many of the Maya gods appear with crossed eyes. Parents hung a small bead from the middle of their child's forehead. This caused the child to look at the object and naturally cross their eyes.

Jewelry and gemstones were a widespread accessory for Maya nobles, both men and women. The most highly valued gemstone was jade; it was green—the color of plants and thus a symbolic color of rebirth—and it was rare. According to archaeologist Charles Gallenkamp, "Older children had their earlobes, septums [tissue that separates the nostrils], lips, and one nostril pierced so they could wear a variety of ornaments."[11] Such piercings were generally performed on the children of the elite when they reached the age of five or six.

Jade necklaces and ear pendants, both worn by men, were two of the most common pieces of jewelry. The necklaces generally featured a pectoral, a larger piece of carved jade made into the necklace and displayed on the upper chest. This emblem signified his family's status and lineage. These necklaces were either passed from father to son or were included in the items buried with a person of great rank. Ear pendants were inserted through the earlobes, with progressively larger and larger inserts, and generally made up of several pieces of ornately carved jade.

Every culture has its own idea of what is considered beautiful and desirable, and the Maya were no different. In cultures with distinct social classes, a person's appearance often shows status, wealth, and position. The ruling elite of the Classic Period reflected that trend. They wore large amounts of jade, quetzal feathers, and obsidian—all relatively rare and expensive items.

The most visible difference between common people and nobility was their outward appearance. Maya commoners tried to imitate the techniques that the nobility used in order to make themselves look beautiful, but they could not afford to go to the extremes that the nobility generally went to in order to look good. Whereas nobles led lives of ease due to extravagant wealth and power, commoners had to work—on the farms, in the quarries, in the workshops, and in the markets. Their simpler lifestyles required simpler clothing, more functional hairstyles, and jewelry and other physical adornments that were less expensive. Although less adorned than the upper class, the commoners were the backbone of the Classic Maya civilization.

This statue—a detail which appears on a door in Palenque, Mexico, from the ninth century—depicts a Maya woman wearing earrings and a necklace to signify wealth.

CHAPTER THREE

COMMON MAYA PEOPLE

The largest group of Maya people during the Classic Period were the commoners. These people were necessary for the survival of the civilization, yet they lived much less glamorous lives than their wealthy counterparts. Most of their days were spent working and farming, and they were truly the people who allowed the Maya nobility to thrive.

Commoners: The Backbone of the Maya Community

During the height of the Classic Period, scholars estimate that around 98 percent of the population must have been commoners, and the majority of commoners were farmers. Without the labor and support of such a large underclass, the Maya nobility could never have achieved such a high level of civilization. However, the lower classes—those who cleared the land, grew the crops, and quarried the stone—were seldom represented in Maya art. Few artifacts have been found belonging to common people, other than stone and bone tools, bits of utilitarian pottery, grinding stones, and the earthen mounds that indicate the former locations of peasant huts.

For that reason, scholars have a severely limited knowledge of Maya commoners during the Classic Period. Many of their theories about the lower classes have been based on the writings of Spaniards such as Diego de Landa. These Spaniards observed firsthand how the Maya lived at the time of the Spanish conquest and during the Colonial Period. Likewise, scholars have also observed how rural Maya peasants live today in Mexico and Central America.

The *Yalba Uinicob*

According to de Landa and others who wrote about the Maya during and after the Spanish conquest, two classes of commoners—*yalba uinicob*, or "lower men"—lived in Classic Maya society.

This artwork shows Maya craftsmen shaping tools. The survival of the civilization depended on skilled laborers and farmers.

The upper level of commoners was made up of skilled artisans and merchants—what might today be considered a middle class; the lower level consisted of unskilled laborers. Skilled artisans and craftsmen included stone and wood carvers, stucco workers, painters, potters, and sculptors. These individuals produced the monuments, murals, and ceramics that had been designed and engineered by members of the *ahau* class. Traders and lower-level bureaucrats were also part of this Maya "middle class."

Merchants and tradesmen—almost always men—bought and sold the goods each city-state produced. They also traveled from place to place, trading with their city-state's neighbors—sometimes hundreds of miles away. Their homes were generally stone, but they were smaller, less ornate, and located farther from the city's center than those of the *ahau* class.

Lower-level commoners were unskilled workers. In rural farming areas, this included primarily farmers, but in urban city areas, they were stonecutters, cleaners, and porters. Farmers wore simple cotton garments and sandals, and they raised food for themselves and to support the king, the royal family, and the nobility. All land was considered the property of the king, as in most feudal societies. During the dry season, many farmers provided labor for the construction of causeways, temples, and palaces. They also cut wood for fuel and timber, but scholars agree it was the food they produced on their farms that was the key to the Maya civilization's success in the region's harsh climate.

Commoner Homes: Simple yet Effective

Most commoners lived on the outskirts of cities or in the jungle. Their homes were simple huts constructed of poles, mud, and plaster with steeply pitched roofs made of palm fronds. Most Maya houses were oval, round, or rectangular, and they were constructed using a wattle-and-daub technique. A row of poles was set in the earth, and mud was packed in between the poles, thus creating thick, solid walls when the mud dried. Inside a typical Maya house, the space was divided into two sections by a tall partition or wall. The front served for everyday activities, and the rear was for sleeping. Other smaller structures often stood near the house, serving as kitchen or storage areas. The entire complex was built atop a low earthen platform to ensure that water drained away from the house.

Because of their simple construction, peasant houses lasted only one generation before being torn down. Each time the resident of a house died, they were buried in the earthen platform on which the house had been standing. The Maya believed that this practice kept the spirits of their ancestors nearby.

A commoner's home had very little furniture. Cooking was done on a stone hearth, generally with ceramic pots. Other kitchen equipment consisted of woven baskets and bags, clay pots, hollowed-out gourd scoops, stone tools, and perhaps wooden chests. Every kitchen also had a metate and a mano—stones specifically used for grinding maize. Stools and benches, constructed by tightly lashing together wooden poles and covering the framework with woven matting, served as seating. Low beds were constructed in much the same way, with woven matting stretched across lashed poles.

Archaeologists can learn a great deal about a family's social standing during the Classic Period by excavating and studying the family's home. Professor Arthur Demarest explained how the location, design, and contents of excavated huts can help scholars understand Maya social classes:

> Some of the social patterns of Classic Maya society were "fossilized" in architecture and artifacts in the ruins of household groups. For each household group the amount of stone masonry (versus mud and thatch) often varied with the social rank of the ancient inhabitants. Height and area of household platforms, the presence or absence of monuments, distance from the nearest epicenter, the number of courtyards, presence of plastered floors, and the types of pottery and artifacts in burials are all clues to the social and political standing of a group's ancient inhabitants.[12]

Cerén

In 1976, a Salvadoran bulldozer operator accidentally bumped into the buried remains of a wall belonging to an ancient Maya house. He notified authorities, work was stopped, and two years later, when excavations began, archaeologists discovered an almost intact farming village from the Maya Classic Period. They believe the village was buried under 17 feet (5 m) of ash when a nearby volcano erupted, probably around AD 600. The site, called Cerén, is located in the Zapotitán Valley, 20 miles (32 km) northwest of El Salvador's capital city, San Salvador. Cerén is providing archaeologists their first peek at a rural Maya village as it existed during that time.

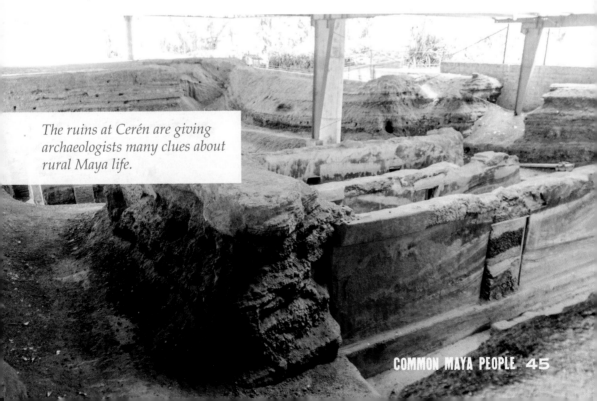

The ruins at Cerén are giving archaeologists many clues about rural Maya life.

Nicknamed "the New World Pompeii," Cerén was carefully excavated by a team of archaeologists from the University of Colorado, Boulder. What they found in the village and the surrounding farmland challenges some of what scholars have theorized about rural peasant life during the Classic Period. The area was apparently covered with volcanic ash fairly rapidly, preserving it just as the eruption of Mount Vesuvius preserved the ancient Roman cities of Pompeii and Herculaneum.

Scientists have not unearthed any human remains at Cerén. The household doors were still tied, and there was no evidence of people going back to their homes to gather belongings. Based on this evidence, scholars believe the villagers fled to the South because the danger was focused in the North. Additionally, huts have been uncovered that still have the occupants' straw bedding tucked into the rafters—just as modern Maya peasants do, to store their bedding out of the way during the

Shown here is an archaeological site made by those studying the ruins at Cerén in El Salvador.

day—indicating the disaster probably occurred during the day. Among the discoveries made at Cerén are clues to how the Maya villagers farmed their land and what crops they grew.

Farming for the Masses

One of the biggest mysteries surrounding the Maya of the Classic Period, until recently, has been how Maya farmers were able to grow enough food from the relatively poor soils of the Yucatán and the highlands of Guatemala to support a population large enough to have built such massive cities.

Studying food production and consumption is often an important piece of understanding ancient cultures, and apparently, Maya farmers excelled at maximizing their food production, even under extremely difficult growing conditions.

Although kings and nobles ate more lavishly, even Maya commoners consumed a balanced diet. For years, scientists thought corn, or maize, made up more than 50 percent of the daily food intake of the Classic Maya—that it alone provided the bulk of their nutrition. It is true that maize was a significant food source, as well as a central element in Maya mythology and frequently a prominent feature of their monumental art. However, scientists have long doubted the Maya could have grown enough maize to feed the populations that are now being attributed to Maya cities of that period.

Recent discoveries at Cerén seem to indicate that another plant—manioc root—may have been just as important to the Maya diet. Payson Sheets, the leader of the group excavating Cerén, believes that what they are finding may change scholars' ideas about which foods kept Classic Maya society going for so long. They found evidence of some corn growing below the thick layer of volcanic ash, but they also found row upon row of once-flourishing manioc plants. It is estimated the manioc field yielded more than 10 tons (9 mt) of manioc shortly before the volcanic eruption.

Manioc, a common root crop in the American tropics today, is a hardy plant that produces a waxy, relatively tasteless root. Its flesh can be made into anything from tortillas to liquor. It is easy to grow, thrives virtually anywhere, has loads of carbohydrates, and provides about six times the calories of an equivalent amount of corn. It is generally boiled and eaten like a potato. It can be grated, fried, turned into flour, or, when sugar is added, made into a dessert. It has long been known that the Maya ate manioc, but it was thought to have been a minor part of their diet. This is largely because, as a root crop, evidence of its cultivation during ancient times is virtually impossible to find. Seeds such as corn might survive centuries

A TREAT FOR THE MAYA

In Mesoamerica, the Maya—commoners and nobility alike—enjoyed a bitter beverage made from cacao beans. Nobles may have had it often, but commoners considered it a luxury because the beans were so rare. The hot chocolate people drink today is generally made with milk and sugar, but neither was used during the time of the Maya. Instead, they mixed cacao with chili peppers, making a spicy, bitter drink. Sometimes they mixed it with ground maize or flavored it with a cinnamon-like bark called canela.

Cacao beans, which come from the pods shown here, were extremely rare and a luxury for the Maya people to enjoy.

under the proper conditions, but not roots.

At Cerén, however, Sheets's team has excavated fields where manioc was grown—carefully weeded and in long, straight, parallel rows to maximize production. The manioc roots themselves are gone, of course, but thanks to the protection of the volcanic ash, cavities in the ground that remained after the roots shriveled away are mostly intact, similar to the cavities that remained after the bodies of those who perished and were buried in Pompeii disintegrated. Excavators carefully filled the manioc cavities with plaster. Once the plaster hardened and was dug up, they produced almost perfect casts of manioc roots.

According to Sheets, "We're seeing what they actually grew, as they grew it. In other places, you might get bits of pollen, small pieces of evidence. Here you see the techniques, the furrows, the farm implements, everything."[13] Although their discoveries have been encouraging, Sheets is quick to point out that finding evidence in a small peripheral Classic Maya location like Cerén does not prove that the growing of manioc took place across all of Maya territory.

What Else Did the Maya Eat?

Despite the implications of the discovery in El Salvador, corn was, and is still, a mainstay of the Maya diet. Besides the ever-present tortilla,

SLASH-AND-BURN FARMING

Maya farmers of the Classic Period used the slash-and-burn, or swidden, method of farming. Underbrush on a particular plot was chopped down with a stone ax, or *bat*, leaving the larger trees for shade and to hold the soil. Eventually—generally in the dry season of late March, April, and May—the then-dry debris was burned, leaving cleared land with a rich layer of carbon and ash to serve as fertilizer on which to plant seeds.

Planting was done by Maya farmers with a simple, fire-hardened digging stick. Heavy rains in June and July germinated and sustained the crops, with a minimum of weeding, until harvest. This method, however—which is still used in much of the world—tends to deplete the soil after only a few years. More land then must be cleared and planted while the original field is allowed to lie unplanted, or fallow, for some years to rebuild its fertility.

the Maya used cornmeal in almost everything they ate or drank. With corn and possibly manioc to provide carbohydrates—sources of energy—they ate beans for protein and squash and chili peppers for essential vitamins. Add to that a few fresh fruits and an occasional bit of meat, and they consumed everything their bodies needed.

Besides their staple foods, the Maya also grew sweet potatoes, tomatoes, avocados, jicama (a root similar to a turnip), papaya, mulberries, melons, and pumpkins. The squash-like fruit of the chayote, a vine that grows all across the Yucatán Peninsula, was also a favorite. Two fruit trees in particular have been associated with Classic Maya sites, so much so that in some cases finding them helps explorers locate remote structures that have been completely covered by jungle. The first is the breadnut or ramon tree, which produces an edible nut enclosed in an edible fruit capsule. The fruit, an important source of protein, was valued by the ancient Maya also because the leaves could be fed to their domesticated animals.

The other tree found quite often around Maya sites is the amapolla tree, prized in part, according to former professor Peter D. Harrison, because it "bears bright red fruit, with no leaves visible. Not only was red a sacred color to the Maya, the color of the East and of the rising sun, which they worshipped as a god, but it came to represent the color of life—possibly because of the association with blood." However, the main reason the Maya valued the amapolla was because its sap, which they could easily collect, could be "fermented to make a highly intoxicating drink."[14]

For meat, the Classic Maya fished and hunted small game such as deer, rabbits, armadillos, birds, turtles, iguanas, and tapirs. They also raised domesticated turkeys, ducks, dogs, and bees. The Maya were skilled beekeepers. They raised bees and housed them near their homes in hollow logs sealed at each end with mud. In addition to using honey as a sweetener, they mixed it with tree bark and fermented it into a popular drink called *balché*.

Besides *balché*, the Maya also loved to drink cacao, generally in the form of a relatively bitter drink mixed with ground corn. The Maya cultivated cacao trees on the Pacific Coast, on the western Yucatán Peninsula north of Belize, and in the lowlands of the Mexican state of Tabasco beginning in the Middle Preclassic Period. The trees are fairly delicate and can grow only under specific climatic conditions. Cacao blooms are pollinated only by mosquitoes, so they thrive in the shade of larger trees. Because of their scarcity, cacao beans were highly prized and traded as far away as central Mexico during the Classic Period, and they were a form of money during the Postclassic Period.

This tablet shows a priest making offerings to a cacao plant. The Maya believed that the gods influenced everything they did, including farming.

Daily Maya Life

The Maya believed that their daily life was controlled by forces that were beyond them that they could not see or understand. Astrology was very important to the Maya, and they believed that things such as the position of stars, movement of planets, and phases of the moon had power over them. Priests had the important job of interpreting the celestial signs for the common people. Priests, for example, would determine when to get married, when to have children, and what to name them.

A child's given name (first name), or *paal kaba*, was carefully chosen during a ceremony conducted by a lower priest. Each child was given four different names—their *paal kaba*, their father's family name, their mother's family name (or *naal kaba*), and finally, an informal nickname, or *coco kaba*. Masculine given names began with the prefix *Ah*, and feminine given names began with *Ix*.

The Maya also had traditions for when children reached a certain age. At about the age of four, girls were given a red shell to be worn on a string tied around their waists until puberty, and boys had a small white bead fastened to their hair. No evidence has been found of formal schools among Maya commoners, but parents taught their children what they needed to know. When boys reached the age of 14 and girls the age of 12, they went through a coming-of-age ceremony, were considered old enough for marriage, and could leave home.

All Maya marriages were arranged, either by a child's father or by an *ah atanzahob*, a professional matchmaker. After the marriage, the groom lived with and worked for the bride's family for six or seven years. At that time, he could build a separate home for his family near his own parents' house.

Women took care of household chores such as collecting firewood, gathering and preparing foods, weaving cloth for clothing, and making household containers from clay, gourds, and other materials. Free time was almost nonexistent, but most families attended public religious ceremonies. Many of these events involved music, with instruments such as drums, flutes, bells, and trumpets. They also might have watched dramatic presentations or plays, with actors presenting stories from their mythology.

As soon as Maya children were around the age of four or five, they joined their parents and put work ahead of play. When they had some free time, children played a board game with beans, or they played with balls made from the elastic gum of rubber trees. Boys ran and chased each other, playing the hunter and the hunted.

The stories of the lives of common people vanished almost as soon as they died. Scholars are fortunate to have the accounts of Diego de Landa and others to tell them about the homes, appearance, clothing, food, and activities of the common Maya at the time of the Spanish conquest, but they can only infer from those sources what life was like for the Maya during the Classic Period.

Scholars are also fortunate that there are new excavations of Maya sites that are still providing a wealth of information, even thousands of years later. These sources, along with the ruins of Maya cities, undisturbed Maya tombs, what remains of the codices, and hieroglyphs carved onto stone monuments, help scholars better understand who the Maya were and what they achieved during their golden age.

While daily life for the Maya common people looks very different from what people are now used to, it was normal for them. Farming, raising a family, household chores, and even the occasional treat governed daily life for the hardworking commoners who helped to keep the civilization flourishing. Commoners may have lived separately from the wealthy nobles, but without them, the civilization would have crumbled.

Ceramics, such as those pictured here, were most likely used for daily chores such as cooking.

CHAPTER FOUR

MAYA LEGACY

The Maya were able to accomplish some amazing things, and scientists today still marvel at what they accomplished, despite their lack of modern technology. From pyramids to cities, farming to astrology, the Maya were truly a people who were ahead of their time.

Long-Lasting Achievements

The Maya left behind many valuable achievements, but the most visible achievements of the ancient Maya are their vast cities and towering pyramids. Advances in architectural design and building techniques helped them create cities and monuments that rivaled those of ancient Mesopotamia, Egypt, Greece, and Rome. Upon closer inspection, though, more subtle inventions and discoveries come to light—discoveries that allowed the Maya civilization to develop to a level that allowed it to design and construct those long-lasting structures.

The Maya built massive architectural wonders that soar above the tree line and are visible from miles away. The site at Tikal (left) is on the United Nations Educational, Scientific and Cultural Organization's (UNESCO) World Heritage List.

Advanced Farming Techniques

Increases in Maya population during the Late Preclassic and Classic periods made it necessary to clear more land and increase production. The Maya built extensive irrigation systems and developed other intensive agricultural practices, such as the construction of terraces on hillsides and raised beds in swampy areas. The practice of terracing made thousands of acres of otherwise unavailable land available to Maya farmers. Terraces of various types—some built during the Classic Period—are still in use today by Guatemalan and Mexican farmers.

A large portion of the Yucatán consists of damp, swampy areas called *bajos*—lowlands—that are unsuitable for normal farming practices. The Petén region in the central lowlands of Guatemala has even less suitable land for farming, with only drier upland areas suitable for the crop rotation of the *milpas* system. To reclaim swampland for farming, the Maya built raised beds for crops. They constructed a checkerboard-like pattern of these raised beds in the *bajos* by scooping mud from the bottom of channels and piling it up between them.

The roughly rectangular man-made islands they created were then used for raising crops. Because the soil was constantly refertilized every time they added more of the organically rich mud, farmers were able to grow some crops year-round, which greatly increased food production. Without such advanced agricultural practices, it would have been impossible to provide enough food to support the number of people required to construct the Maya's most visible achievement—stone cities.

Limestone Blocks

Cities built by the Maya in the Late Preclassic, Classic, and Postclassic periods reflect advanced intelligence and craftsmanship. The city-state of Tikal, for example, may have covered 47 square miles (122 sq km) during its golden age, with a "downtown" area of 6 square miles (16 sq km). Towering over Tikal's central Great Plaza are numerous stone pyramids—tombs of their kings—and two massive stone pyramid-temples, Temple I and Temple II, are on each side. Like most Maya pyramids, these were built using limestone found in quarries nearby.

Limestone is relatively soft and easy to cut into blocks while still in the ground. It hardens after being exposed to air. During the Late Preclassic Period, the Maya discovered that they could cut grooves into the natural limestone rock with flint or obsidian tools, deepen the grooves, and eventually use levers and wedges to separate a stone block.

Then, while the limestone block was still damp, they carved it roughly into the shape they needed using wooden hammers or hammer stones and stone chisels. Workers used a wooden sled to transport the block to the building site, where craftsmen finished carving and polishing it. If the limestone was particularly soft, as it was near Palenque, craftsmen used a special twin-bladed stone knife to complete the carving.

Achievements in Building

Pyramids such as those at Tikal and Palenque, along with hundreds of others in cities such as Piedras Negras, Quiriguá, and Copán, reflect two advancements in architecture and building techniques similar in some ways to those of the Roman Empire—the arch and cement. The Maya developed the use of arches in their construction, but theirs were not true arches, such as those built by the Romans. Instead, the Maya built corbelled arches for many of their doorways and high ceilings for many of the pyramids' rooms. A corbelled arch is made when stones forming layers, or courses, on opposite walls are extended gradually toward the center of the open space. Each course sticks farther out into the space until the opposite walls meet, forming a triangularly shaped ceiling with a capstone on top, connecting the sides. Because this type of arch cannot span much open space without collapsing, rooms topped with them had to be somewhat narrow.

Some of the most recognizable achievements of the Maya civilization are their huge buildings, such as those seen at Palenque.

Like arches, Maya cement also differed in some ways from what the Romans used, yet it served the same purposes: mortar or "glue" to attach stone to stone in a wall and stucco to seal the surfaces of structures and decorate their walls with raised images and hieroglyphs. The Maya burned limestone, pulverized it, and mixed it into a substance similar to cement. The mixture formed a bond so tight that stones joined with it seemed to be naturally joined—as if the structures were made of one piece of stone. During the Middle and Late Preclassic periods, the Maya used stucco to decorate the walls and steps of their buildings, generally with three-dimensional images from their mythology.

Maya Pyramids

All Maya pyramids share certain characteristics. They are step pyramids rather than smooth-sided "true" pyramids like the Great Pyramid of Egypt, and all are topped by other structures. Maya pyramids, in general, have three components: a stepped pyramidal base with a stairway leading to the top, a chambered sanctuary or temple atop the pyramid, and a decorative masonry "topknot"—called a roof comb—stretching skyward from the roof of the temple. Though they serve no practical purpose, these roof combs give Classic Maya pyramids their distinctive look. Scholars believe they were added to Classic Period pyramids to increase their height and make them appear larger, more sacred, and closer to the heavens.

Temple III at Tikal stretches high above the tree line as shown here. This is an amazing architectural accomplishment.

At Tikal—"City of Echoes" in Mayan—sit six large pyramids with roof combs. Filmmaker George Lucas was so impressed with these pyramids in Tikal that he used its skyline as a backdrop for several scenes in the 1977 movie *Star Wars: A New Hope*. Pyramids at Palenque, a Maya site in the Mexican state of Chiapas, all have unique roof combs. Instead of the solid roof combs of Tikal, each Palenque structure is topped with a latticed roof comb carved with scenes from Maya mythology.

Maya pyramids make up the majority of structures in the central areas of Maya cities. Whereas some served as tombs, others were foundations for temples, astronomical observatories, or other government buildings. Thanks to hieroglyphic carvings on the structures, archaeologists generally are able to determine when each was built and by whom. What archaeologists do not know is how many more Maya pyramids remain undiscovered in the dense jungles of the Yucatán Peninsula and Central American highlands, mistaken for tree- and vine-covered hills.

Some Maya pyramids are buried beneath other pyramids that were built at a later date. It was common practice among Maya kings in the Classic Period to build a larger pyramid over one that had already been built, often using the older structure as the foundation for the new one. In some cases, the pyramids are stacked one inside the other. For example, Temple 26 in Copán, Honduras, sits atop at least 6 previously built pyramids. Scholars can literally dig their way through the history of the city and its kings.

Often, these "stacked" pyramids each contain a king's tomb, allowing excavators to see how each dynasty differed from those that came before it. Many of the covered structures were carefully preserved in the process, protecting them from the elements. As each layer of the new pyramid was laid in place, workers carefully packed sand between the new structure and the old, covering the carvings on the older pyramid to form a solid core for the new structure. Archaeologists tunnel into pyramids, remove the sand, and study the carvings and hieroglyphs on older pyramids.

Some pyramids are in well-known ceremonial centers, such as Tikal, Copán, Uxmal, Palenque, and Chichén Itzá, while others are in lesser-known, more recently discovered sites. Some Maya pyramids are simple platforms on which temples were built; others are steep, ornate structures with many levels. Many contain tombs, such as the Pyramid of the Inscriptions at Palenque and Temple I at Tikal, but others do not.

Some pyramids were used as foundations for astronomical observatories. El Caracol at Chichén Itzá in the northern Yucatán is one example of this. This structure is one of the few round Maya structures and was built atop a step pyramid to elevate it above the surrounding terrain for observation of the rising and setting of the sun, the moon, the planet Venus, and other heavenly bodies. El Caracol, which means "the snail" in Spanish, was named for its internal spiral staircase, which resembles the pattern on a snail's shell.

Paintings and carvings on temple walls, pyramids and other structures, ceramic pottery, and stelae depict scenes of life in every Maya city. Alongside these paintings and sculptures are thousands of smaller carvings that early archaeologists recognized as a form of hieroglyphic writing. For centuries, no one knew what the Maya had written, but today they do.

The Maya's Written Language

Other civilizations in the New World recorded their history, mythology, and sometimes their business transactions, but the Maya were the only ones in the Western Hemisphere to develop a complete, complex system of writing. It was so complex that more than 50 years ago, no scholar could read it. Now the secrets of the Maya's written language are gradually coming to light.

Like the ancient Egyptians, the Maya incorporated pictograms into their system of writing. A pictogram is a picture that represents an object. For example, to convey the word "snake," the Maya drew a small snake, generally stylized within a roughly square image. Had their written language used only pictograms and number symbols, they could

have recorded basic stories about events that occurred around them, but if they had wanted to write "air," for example, or "beauty," pictograms would have been far too limiting.

To improve their written language, the Maya developed symbols called ideograms to represent nonphysical concepts. They had symbols for concepts such as love, hate, anger, and pride. The use of ideograms allowed them more freedom of expression, but they also wanted to express the sounds of their spoken language. They therefore developed symbols called syllabograms to represent sounds. Each syllabogram contained one consonant and one vowel; like English, a vowel could be pronounced more than one way, so the Maya devised different syllabograms for each pronunciation.

Due to its use of pictograms (also called logograms or "word signs") and syllabograms, Maya writing is referred to as a logosyllabic language, or a mixed system. More than 800 writing signs have been identified so far, and most can now be read, allowing scholars to understand specific details about the Maya—such as names, places, and concepts—they could not read before.

Maya hieroglyphic texts are read from left to right, top to bottom, two glyphs at a time. As scholar Heather McKillop explained, "To read a glyphic text on a Classic stela, for example, one begins at the top left corner, reads the first two glyphs, and then continues reading glyphs below them, by pairs. Once at the bottom, one returns to the top of the text and reads the next column of glyphs, again by pairs."[15]

Today, scholars can read most of what they find in Maya cities, revolutionizing the study of this ancient civilization. According to Michael D. Coe,

The history of the American continent does not begin with Christopher Columbus, or even with Leif the Lucky, but with those Maya scribes in the Central American jungles who first began to record the deeds of their rulers some two thousand years ago. Of all the peoples of the pre-Columbian New World, only the ancient Maya had a complete script: they could write down anything they wanted to, in their own language.

During the nineteenth century, following the discovery of the ruined Maya cities, almost none of these records could be read by Western scholars ...Today, thanks to some remarkable advances made by epigraphers [those who decipher hieroglyphics] on both sides of the Atlantic, we can now read most of what those long-dead scribes carved on their stone monuments.

I believe that this decipherment is one of the most exciting adventures of our age, on a par with the exploration of space and the discovery of the genetic code.[16]

The Maya written language is made of a series of pictograms, which were generally created within a square, such as those shown here.

The late Linda Schele of the University of Texas, who interpreted and read Maya glyphs, said, "Those glyphs give the Maya 1,500 years of history, written in the words of their ancestors, not in the words of white people from Europe."[17] Simon Martin, another epigrapher and the coauthor of several books on the Maya, added, "This is our one and only opportunity to peer into the Americas before the arrival of Europeans and hear these people speaking to us … [It gives] us an indigenous insight into what they thought was important."[18]

One thing the Maya thought was important was the study of astronomy. Much of what the Maya wrote—on stelae, ceramic pottery, and temple walls—involved what they observed and predicted, based on studying the stars.

Studying the Skies

In cities throughout the Yucatán, alongside pyramids, ball courts, and temples, the Maya built observatories to watch the skies. The Maya gods were thought to reside in the heavens, so worship included watching the sky. Centuries of watching the sun, moon, and stars rise above the horizon eventually led the Maya to develop a sophisticated astronomy. Early scholars noticed that the location from which the heavenly bodies emerged on the horizon varied depending on the season. They studied the phenomenon by driving two stakes in the ground or by placing two vertical stones to align them with the location on the horizon of those celestial events.

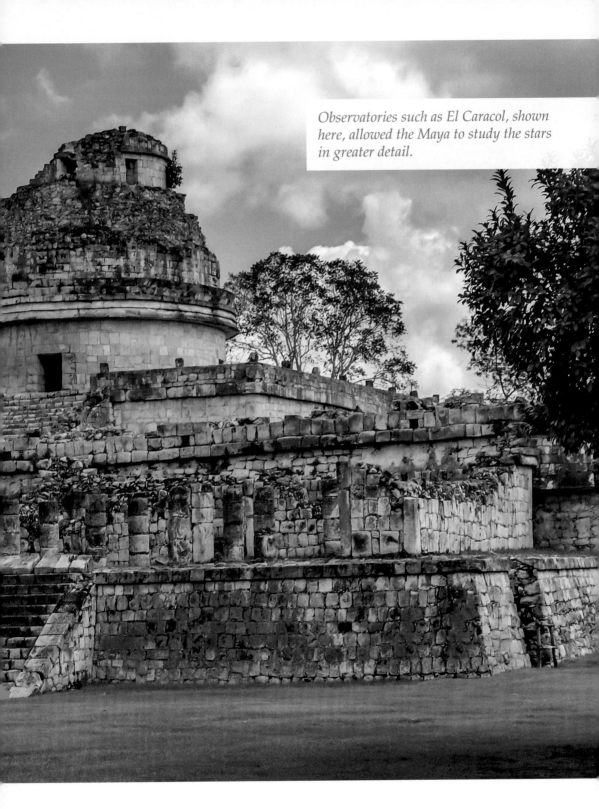

Observatories such as El Caracol, shown here, allowed the Maya to study the stars in greater detail.

Over time, they noticed repeating patterns that made it possible for them to predict when certain events would occur. They eventually built stone observatories with windows aligned with those points; this allowed them greater accuracy in their predictions.

During the Late Preclassic and Classic periods, the Maya built pyramids and plazas along astronomical lines. They aligned these structures with the path of the sun on certain days of the year or with the cardinal directions (North, South, East, and West). At many of these pyramids, a person standing at the entrance of the temple could look out over the surrounding smaller pyramids and see the sun rise directly over one pyramid on the summer solstice, over another on both the fall and spring equinoxes, and over yet another on the winter solstice.

Some sites, however, did not align their structures with the path of the sun. Instead, they aligned them with the paths of other celestial bodies. One example is at Tak'alik Ab'aj ("Standing Stones"), a Late Preclassic site near the Pacific Coast of western Guatemala. Scholars believe its builders aligned the structures with the star Eta Draconis in the dragon-shaped constellation Draco.

Maya astronomers achieved a remarkable degree of accuracy without the technology society has today. They were able to chart the movement of stars and planets. Using only fixed lines of sight, crossed sticks, and fixed observation points, Maya astronomers and mathematicians calculated the length of a year on Earth to be 365.2420 days, incredibly close to the actual figure of 365.2422. They were also able to predict the changing of seasons, the arrival of comets, and the occurrences of solar and lunar eclipses.

Math and Time

The Maya's intense study of astronomy required the development of an equally complex system of mathematics in order to help with their study of the heavens and skies. Theirs was vigesimal, based on the number 20, rather than decimal, based on 10. They also developed the concept of zero, possibly as early as 36 BC. Although it seems basic to modern cultures, zero is a relatively complicated mathematical idea. It was unknown in Europe until the Middle Ages, when the idea finally found its way from India, by way of the Arabian Peninsula. No symbol for zero appears in Roman numerals because the Romans did not consider it necessary to have a numeral to represent nothing. However, advanced mathematics would be useless without the concept of zero.

Both astronomy and mathematics were essential for the Maya's true focus—time. No ancient civilization, in the Old World or the New, was more focused on the passage of time than the Maya. Mathematics and astronomy were tools for the creation of the most important technological advancement for the Maya—their calendar. Almost 1,200 years before the adoption of the

Gregorian calendar that most of the world uses today, the more accurate Maya calendar was in use.

The Maya became focused on their calendar as part of their religious observances. The Maya's numerous gods and goddesses were believed to live in the heavens and embodied certain stars, moons, and planets. Therefore, studying and anticipating the repeating cycles of these celestial bodies became an important practice to develop and maintain a calendar. The Maya believed that the passage of time controlled the universe. Anthropologist Alexander W. Voss explained why the Maya calendar was so closely associated with their gods: "In a never-ending cycle [the gods] were born, developed their powers and then died, only to be born again at a precisely determined time and start a new cycle. To the Maya, these supernatural entities represented time and were responsible for maintaining cosmic order."[19]

Although some other ancient calendars that can be viewed, such as this one, might be based on the Maya calendar, a complete physical Maya calendar has never been found.

RECREATION AND GAMES

The Mesoamerican ball game, played in specially constructed courts in virtually every Maya city throughout their history, was possibly the foundation for the modern games of football, soccer, basketball, volleyball, and other ball games. Based on fragmentary evidence, scholars believe it was played as either a team sport or an individual competition by both men and women. Players wore protective clothing, including headgear, knee pads, and quilted cotton armor. Some wore what the Spanish called a yugo, which was a heavy wooden shield in the shape of a horseshoe that was worn around the stomach.

The ball—varying in size up to 12 inches (30 cm) in diameter—was made from latex obtained from local rubber trees. It was relatively hard and could weigh as much as 8 pounds (3.6 kg). Once the ball was tossed into play, it was hit back and forth only with the hips, thighs, or upper arms. The ultimate goal was to put the ball through a ring. Maya kings often played the game to symbolically reenact scenes from the Maya creation myth.

Hoops, such as the one shown here, were found at the Chichén Itzá archaeological site. These hoops were part of a game played for fun and to reenact a creation myth.

Because these cycles were thought to be necessary to their survival, observing certain religious ceremonies on certain days of the year was also thought to be crucial. Using their calendar each day, they predicted important events and calculated which supernatural being, good or evil, would rule that day. They then performed ceremonies they felt would best influence the cosmic entity in their favor.

A Very Advanced Calendar

The passage of time was central to the Maya way of life. Maya scribes listed dates on almost every painting, stela, and ceramic vase they created, but they never seem to have carved or otherwise depicted their entire complex calendar. Some sources suggest that the circular stone calendar of the Aztecs—sometimes referred to as the Aztec Sun Stone—also represented the Maya calendar, but the two are totally different. The Maya calendar was actually three separate calendars that ran at the same time, and no graphical depiction of all three has been discovered.

In addition to a complex and accurate calendar, the Maya studied lunar cycles to predict lunar and solar eclipses. They also were focused on the planet Venus, which they associated with war. Alexander W. Voss explained that the Maya considered Venus "a bringer of misfortune, bad omens, and war,"[20] so they had a calendar to predict its position in the sky. Many extensive battles between city-states, the deaths of kings, and the fall of dynasties took place during the rising of the planet Venus.

To the Maya, time ran in cycles. Whatever happened in a particular year or time of year was bound to happen again. The ancient Maya did not see time as merely a means of arranging events in order. Time had mystical significance. In their minds, a different god ruled over each period of time (for example, a month in current timekeeping), and they had to know which god to worship at the appropriate time. Because not all Maya gods were kind toward humanity, some time periods were more dangerous than others.

Religion was central to everything the Maya did. Their pyramids were built high so that they could get closer to the heavens. They studied the stars to learn about their gods and how to worship them. Their games imitated the actions of their gods. Even their food was raised and grown to link them to the gods. The calendar told the Maya which god or goddess they should pray to or make offerings to on a particular day.

Advancements in building, record keeping, and even recreation and games truly helped to define the Maya civilization. It is amazing to see how advanced these people were, despite the fact that they lived so long ago. Even today, scholars continue to be fascinated by the Maya's study of astrology and their precise calendar system.

CHAPTER FIVE

SPIRITS AND THE UNIVERSE

While the daily life of the Maya is fascinating, perhaps even more intriguing are their religious practices, views of the afterlife, and connection with gods and spirits. Everything the Maya did was connected to religion, and they planned their calendar, marriages, planting seasons, and even what they named their children based on pleasing their many gods. Through careful study of artifacts left behind, scholars can begin to piece together exactly what the Maya believed and how it influenced their lives.

Importance of the Calendar

Just as everyday life for the ancient Maya was influenced by their calendar—such as when to plant and harvest crops or when to attend public ceremonies—so were their religious beliefs and practices. The Maya believed time was an important part of how the cosmos functioned. It was crucial for their religious ceremonies to be appropriately timed. Their calendar—and its associated mythology—was a window to the distant past and to the future. It gave the Maya a connection to the previous universe and the evils that led to its destruction, to the creation of this current universe, to its eventual destruction, and to the creation of the next universe.

Heaven and Earth

The Maya had an elaborate view of the heavens, Earth, and Xibalba—what they called the underworld—and how events were interconnected in each level of the universe. They believed the heavens were divided into 13 levels, each with a specific god ruling over it. They believed Xibalba, the "Place of Fright," contained nine levels; each of those levels was presided over by a different, often terrifying, deity. The Maya did not conceive of the underworld as necessarily a place where immoral or evil people went when they died. It was where all people went, except those who died a violent death. All who went to Xibalba had to face tricky challenges from the gods of the underworld. If a soul was successful in outwitting those gods, it ultimately rose into the sky as a heavenly body.

Only those who met a violent death would enter some level of Heaven. These souls went to the level of Heaven presided over by the god who ruled the element of nature that led to their deaths. A person who was struck by lightning or drowned, for example, went to the level ruled by Chaak, the god of rain, thunder, and lightning. War casualties and sacrificial victims went to the level reigned over by K'inich Ajaw, the god of war and blood sacrifice.

Gods in the heavens and in the underworld were said to control what happened on Earth, including rain, the seasons, and sunrises. Kings and priests performed ceremonies and blood sacrifices to nurture the gods and strengthen them for those tasks. This belief in the interconnectedness of the universe, seen and unseen, affected not only the Maya's daily lives but also how they built their homes, laid out their *milpas*, and constructed their cities. The orientation and design of buildings and plazas and the construction of main roads and causeways reflected this focus on imitating on Earth the order and structure they perceived in the universe.

The Maya conceived of Earth as a flat square. Each of its four sides faced a cardinal direction, and each had its own color—red for East, white for North, black for West, yellow for South, and

This depiction of the sun god K'inich Ajaw is just one of the many examples of ways that the Maya honored their gods.

blue-green at the center. Earth was held up at each corner by four ancient gods, above the ocean from which it rose at the moment of creation. The corners of Earth were the points at which the sun rose and set on the summer and winter solstices. At the center of each side lay a mythical mountain with a cave. These were entrances to Xibalba and the ocean. The water above which Earth floated was a link with the underworld. Another Maya source shows Earth resting on the back of a monstrous crocodile, floating in a pond of water lilies.

The Maya believed that honoring the cardinal directions was important, that mountains connected Earth to the heavens, and that caves and cenotes—natural sacred wells—linked Earth to the ocean below. Pyramids represented mountains, and temple doorways represented caves—symbolic entrances to the underworld. Entering a cave or a temple doorway was symbolic of direct contact with the gods. Many major temple complexes in the lowlands of the Yucatán were built directly over caves, and sacrificial altars have been discovered in many caves in the region.

Many cities in the Yucatán were also built near deep circular-shaped cenotes, into which sacrifices to the gods were often thrown. Diego de Landa reported that, in times of drought, the Yucatán Maya threw people into the cenote near Chichén Itzá. When confronted about this, they insisted that the individuals who had been cast in were not dead, even though they were never seen

again. The Maya believed that those sacrificial victims had simply entered the underworld through the cenote and were still alive there.

In the Maya universe, the sky was supported by either another set of four gods or four huge trees, depending

Cenotes, such as this one near Chichén Itzá, were important and sacred to the Maya.

on the source consulted. In the center, serving as an axis to connect the upper world (the heavens), the middle world (Earth), and the underworld, stood either a stalk of maize or a huge ceiba tree—the World Tree. The ceiba, or silk-cotton tree, is the tallest tree in the Maya region of Mesoamerica, reaching a height of 230 feet (70 m). Called *yaxche* ("first tree") in Mayan, they are sacred and are never cut down when farmers clear land for planting.

A stylized image of the World Tree was carved on the rear wall of the sanctuary in the Temple of the Cross at Palenque. The temple was named for the cross-shaped World Tree in the bas-relief carving; the tree is pictured growing out of a sacrificial bowl with the great bird of heaven—Itzam Ye—sitting at its highest point. Itzam Ye was one symbolic form of the Maya's supreme deity, the creator god Itzamna.

The Maya Creation Story

The core of the Maya religion—and the primary reason behind their rituals—was their creation story. The Maya believed humans were created to serve and nurture the gods, and they acted accordingly. During virtually every religious ceremony, Maya kings and queens symbolically reenacted the creation story, reinforcing that belief in their subjects.

The Maya creation story must be pieced together from several sources. Inscriptions in three temples in Palenque, including the one in the Temple of the Cross, provide many details. Similar inscriptions have been found in temples in Quiriguá, Piedras Negras, Cobá, and Copán. Accounts are also found in the *Popol Vuh (The Council Book or The Book of Counsel)*, a 16th-century Maya text that retells their ancient creation story, and in *The Books of Chilam Balam (Books of the Jaguar Prophet)*, a series of 12 books written by Maya village priests after the Spanish conquest.

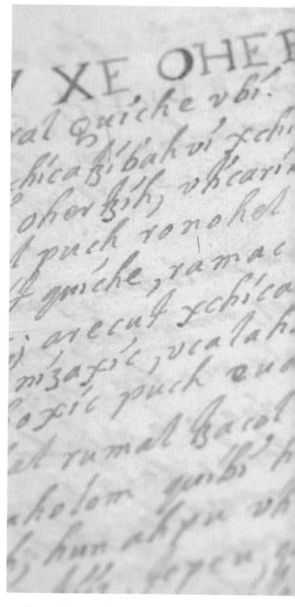

According to these sources, the world as it exists today was created on the Maya date 4 Ajaw 8 Kumk'u—September 8, 3114 BC—but it was not the first to have existed. The previous world and its inhabitants were destroyed by a great flood, followed by a time of semidarkness.

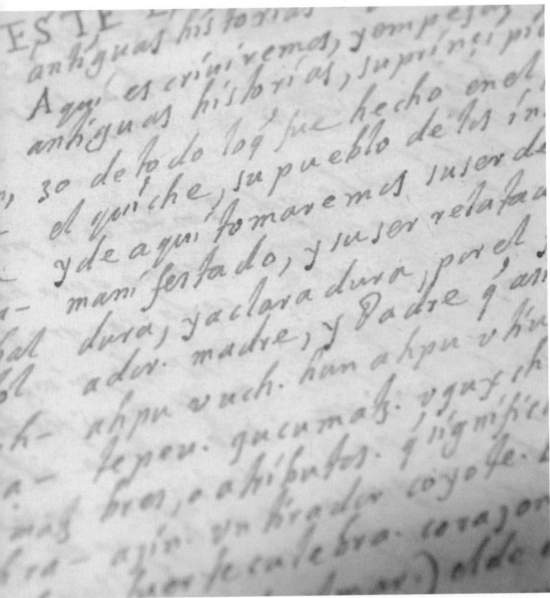

Shown here is an excerpt from the Popol Vuh, *a text that tells the story of the creation of humans.*

During that twilight time, four heroic figures emerged in the cosmos—the Hero Twins (Junajpu and Xb'alanke), their father (Jun Junajpu), and their uncle, Wuqub' Junajpu. Their adventures in Xibalba, vanquishing the evil forces that ruled the early world, were thought to prepare the way for humanity. Their story also explains the importance of the Mesoamerican ball game to the Maya culture.

The Hero Twins

The *Popol Vuh* tells the story of two sets of twins who lived before humanity came into existence. The first twins—sons of the gods Itzamna and Ix Chel—were Jun Junajpu ("One Blowgun") and Wuqub' Junajpu ("Seven Blowgun"). They were skilled ballplayers, but their loud play irritated the lords of the underworld, who invited them to Xibalba for a game. There, the lords challenged them to a series of clever tests. They failed each one and were sacrificed.

Before burying their bodies, the gods decapitated Jun Junajpu, turned his head into a gourd, and placed it in the fork of a tree. When a young woman approached the gourd, it spat into her hand and magically made her pregnant; she then fled Xibalba to the upper world. There, she gave birth to two boys, called the Hero Twins—Junajpu ("Blowgun") and Xb'alanke ("Jaguar"). When the twins were grown, their loud ball playing also irritated the gods of the underworld, and they were summoned below. Unlike their father and uncle, they won each challenge, outwitting the underworld lords and killing them. They resurrected their ancestors and returned with them to the upper world. The rebirth of their father, Jun Junajpu, transformed him into the maize god, a handsome young figure whose life, death, and rebirth was forever associated with the growth cycle of corn and a central element of worship for the Maya.

IMPORTANT BOOKS

For centuries, scholars have been poring over three surviving Maya books—the Dresden Codex, the Madrid Codex, and the Paris Codex. In 1739, the director of the Royal Library of Dresden purchased a codex from a private collector. How and when the collector obtained it is a mystery. The 78-page book, which is the most complete of the codices, contains astronomical tables dealing with the movements of the moon and the planet Venus. The codex became known as the Dresden Codex. The Madrid Codex, a 112-page book, was discovered in Madrid in the 1860s. It is the longest of the surviving codices, containing more than 250 almanacs. The Paris Codex first appeared in France in 1832. It is in very poor condition. The 22 pages of the codex that have survived contain prophecies and astrological information.

A fourth Maya codex, a 10-page fragment called the Codex Grolier, was reportedly found in 1965 in a dry cave in southern Chiapas, Mexico. Its hieroglyphs deal exclusively with astronomical calculations associated with Venus. Although the authenticity of the codex was challenged for decades, in 2016, scholars from Brown University reevaluated the codex and confirmed it was not only authentic but also the oldest known manuscript of the Americas.

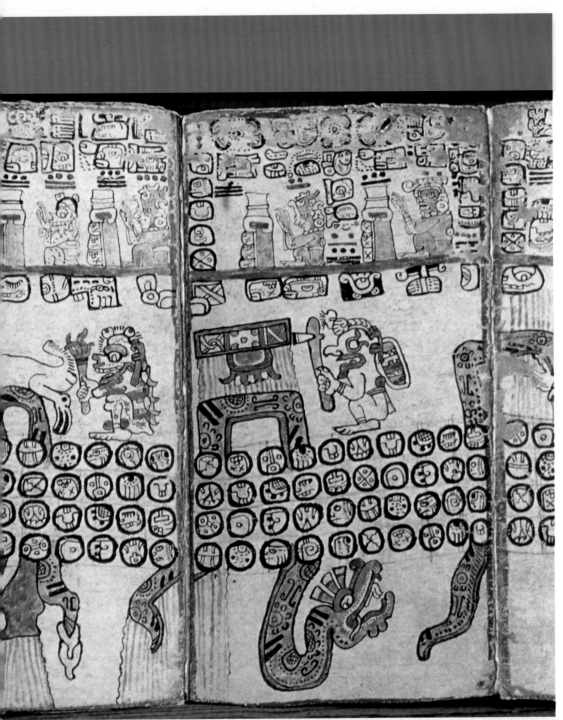

The Madrid Codex, shown here, is the longest Maya codex.

The Hero Twins' victory over the lords of Xibalba served to lessen humanity's dread of the underworld and established the necessity of making offerings to the gods to honor them. Their quest complete, the twins were taken into the sky, where one later became the sun and the other the moon.

Once the evil of the underworld was destroyed, the world experienced a time of twilight. Itzamna, or First Father—the creator god, supreme deity, and inventor of writing—raised the sky above Earth and placed the World Tree at its center. He caused the sky to rotate, which gave Earth life. Plants sprouted from the soil, including maize, which First Mother ground into meal and mixed with water to make a paste. The creator gods formed humans from the maize paste. The new Maize People, as they were called, honored the gods while they waited for the first sunrise. It was a long time coming, and the humans began to lose hope. They wandered aimlessly in the semidarkness until the arrival of a one-legged lightning god named Tojil (sometimes called K'awiil, depicted with a serpent for one leg and a torch sticking out from his forehead).

Tojil brought fire to humans but demanded human sacrifice in return. When the dawn finally arrived, the humans burned incense in gratitude, but it was not enough. The gods made the sun so strong that everything dried out, withering the plants. Tojil again demanded blood offerings, so the early Maya offered animal blood. Still not satisfied, Tojil insisted that human blood be offered. The humans reluctantly followed his orders and offered a human heart. From that time forward, the Maya believed it was their duty to offer human blood to satisfy their gods.

The Confusing World of Maya Gods

Little is known about the Maya gods and goddesses because sources differ. Codices dating from before the Spanish conquest mention 30 deities by name; however, an 18th-century manuscript lists 166. Part of the confusion comes from Maya gods being multifaceted, with more than one appearance, power, or name.

Two or more Maya gods were sometimes combined, as with Tojil, the god of lightning and thunder, and Chaak, the rain god, depicted in some temple images as a single being with characteristics of both gods. A particular god might be pictured as masculine or feminine, young or old, fleshed or skeletal. Each celestial god also had an underworld identity, assumed when it passed beneath Earth on its way to rebirth in the eastern sky.

Maya gods were sometimes shown as infants or small children, cradled in the arms of a mortal king. This image served to reinforce the nobility's unique bond with the gods and their vital role in nurturing those gods with blood sacrifices. Anthropology professor Karl Taub described the relationship depicted in such images: "The act of blood sacrifice ... was tantamount to nurturing the gods ... The Maya kings saw themselves as caring parents of the gods. The gods were looked after and kept alive thanks to the religious activities of the elites."[21]

How Did the Maya Gods Appear?

The Maya worshipped many gods. They believed every living thing had a spirit, with a god or goddess ruling over everything in nature. Local shrines to these numerous gods were called *waybil*, which means "place of sleep." From time to time, the gods had to be awakened and summoned to action. Despite differences between individual Maya city-states across Mesoamerica, as well as changes in beliefs and practices across the centuries of the Maya civilization, the portrayal of certain primary deities remained constant. The roles and importance of individual gods, however, varied, depending on the specific Maya dynasty worshipping them.

Several Maya gods and goddesses remained standard in appearance in images throughout the Maya region and across the centuries. The most prominent was the supreme deity, Itzamna. Because of his extreme age, he was generally portrayed as an ancient figure with a wrinkled face, a hooked nose, and large square eyes resembling goggles. He was pictured wearing a headdress made of a shell that stuck out from his forehead and a headband

with a mirror in the shape of a flower. A pearl-studded strip emerged from the flower mirror, representing nectar or dew. The Maya associated Itzamna with the morning dew and collected it each day from leaves to use as sacred water in ceremonies.

Ix Chel, "Lady Rainbow," also known as Chak Chel, was Itzamna's wife and the most important Maya goddess. She ruled the night sky as goddess of the moon and water. Depicted with a wrinkled face and a long, hooked nose like her husband, she was associated with weaving, medicine, and childbirth. Sometimes, she was pictured as an old, fearsome goddess, with snakes for hair, jaguar claws for hands, and a skirt featuring skulls and crossbones. At other times, she was a beautiful, scantily clad young goddess linked with love and fertility.

K'inich Ajaw, "Sun-faced Lord," was the sun god, one of the most powerful Maya gods. A royal figure, associated with nobles, war, and sacrifice, his worship included ritual war dances and blood sacrifice. He was pictured with beard stubble on a wrinkled face and the Maya hieroglyph *k'in* (sun) on his body. Images of his face adorn the facades of several Classic Period temples. Each night, he transformed into a jaguar to travel through Xibalba.

Chaak, the rain god, was deeply respected by Mesoamerican civilizations dating back to the Olmec and was shared by many cultures in the region. Associated with the cardinal directions,

Itzamna, the creator god, is depicted in this carving in the form of the wise man with a hooked nose.

he ruled lightning, thunder, and rain. Chaak was generally represented with a long, hooked nose and either an axe or a snake in his hand. Today's Maya farmers still make offerings to Chaak.

The maize god was also called Yum Kaax, or Jun Ye Nal, "First Corn Cob." His origin was linked to the resurrection of Jun Junajpu, the father of the Hero Twins. A young man with a remarkably handsome face, the top of his head was sometimes shown as an ear of maize. According to scholar Heather McKillop, "[Jun Junajpu's] death by decapitation is a metaphor for the harvesting of corn and for death."[22] In later murals, the maize god is sometimes shown as a youthful figure diving headfirst from the sky.

The primary god of death for the Maya was Yum Cimil, sometimes called Kimi. He ruled the lowest level of Xibalba. Though sometimes pictured as a fearsome skeletal god, he is also depicted as a comical, grotesque figure who has a huge protruding stomach and dances wildly. Due to the Hero Twins' victory in Xibalba, it appears that the Maya did not always look at Yum Cimil with fear. Sometimes they made fun of him, knowing he could be deceived with rituals and clever tricks.

Rituals and Ceremonies

To keep the universe running as it should and prevent disasters or the end of the world, Maya gods had to be happy. Rituals, including blood sacrifice and vision quests, thus had to be performed on a regular schedule. When something bad happened—a drought or a flood, for example—it was seen as the action of an angry god who felt neglected or insulted.

Religious rituals took place every day, both in peasant huts and on the steps of great stone temples. In Maya homes, a mother offered bits of tortilla to Ix Chel for the health of her child. Before beginning his chores, a farmer burned incense and prayed to Chaak to bring rain to his fields. Some ceremonies involved offering food, tobacco, or alcoholic beverages to the gods. Others involved the most precious of offerings—life itself.

The sacred essence of life, called *k'uhlel*, was the blood of living things. Offering *k'uhlel* to the gods was necessary to preserve the universe. The soul inhabited the heart, according to the Maya. Blood was the essence of the soul, making the heart the ultimate sacrifice. The type of sacrifice offered depended on the importance of the event. The offering might be small birds, animals, or human blood. Among the Maya, human sacrifice was not common, but ritual bloodletting formed an important part of religious ceremonies. Major events, such as the crowning of a new ruler, a natural disaster, a war, or the dedication of a new temple or ball court, required human sacrifice.

For years, archaeologists knew the Maya offered their own blood as an offering to the gods, but they believed the Maya had not practiced human sacrifice until late in their history—near the end of the Postclassic Period. In 1946, however, with the discovery of the Maya city of Bonampak, these theories changed. Murals and sculptures found there—dated between AD 600 and 800—proved the Maya practiced human sacrifice to please their gods. Recent discoveries and the continuing decoding of Maya hieroglyphics also reveal a higher level of blood sacrifice throughout Maya history than previously thought.

Blood for the Gods

Blood was an important part of sacrifice, and both noble and common Maya people often pierced themselves with stingray spines or cut themselves to provide blood for the sacrifice. Diego de Landa described rituals he witnessed in the Yucatán: "They offered sacrifices with their own blood, sometimes … from their ears. Their scarred ears remained as a symbol. On other occasions, they pierced holes in their cheeks and lower lips."[23]

Sacrifice was important to the Maya's worship of their gods. A successful warrior is shown here in this art from Chichén Itzá.

Sometimes Maya priests or nobles wished to seek the gods' advice, and they entered a trancelike state to do so. The Maya believed that these trances allowed them to communicate directly with their gods. Scholar Arthur Demarest described how this was accomplished:

> Ancient shamans, priests, and rulers induced their visions with the aid of massive blood loss which naturally releases opiates in the brain. They also smoked powerful tobacco mixtures or drew upon the rain forest's natural bounty of psychotropic substances. Hallucinogens made from mushrooms were used, and perhaps extracts from morning-glories, water lilies, or the glands of reptiles.[24]

During the Classic Period, many prisoners of war—always men—were also sacrificed. Captured kings often were decapitated. Other prisoners were paraded through the streets in humiliation. Some captives were imprisoned, tortured, and publicly humiliated for years before being sacrificed. The heads of decapitated victims were generally impaled on poles in the plaza or kept in the palace as trophies and buried in the tombs of dead rulers. Captured women were sold as slaves. The Maya were very serious about their sacrifices to the gods and would do whatever it took to ensure that they were making their gods happy.

The Classic Maya: Still a Partial Mystery

Artifacts, stelae, and other written descriptions of the Maya, especially surrounding their religious rituals, have given scholars a vast amount of information about this fascinating society, but many sources have unfortunately been lost to history. Scholars continue to search for answers to learn why the Maya society changed so drastically between the end of the Classic period in 900 and the arrival of the Spanish in the 1500s.

THE MAYA TODAY

The causes of the ancient Maya civilization's decline have been debated for centuries. Some early scholars thought it was caused by a sudden catastrophic event such as an earthquake, a volcanic eruption, or a particularly destructive hurricane. Others believe that there was a large-scale revolt, invasion, or ongoing warfare. Some suspect an epidemic wiped out a large part of the population. Today, scholars have more information based on findings from radiocarbon dating that shed light on reasons for the decline of the Maya people.

The ancient Maya culture may have largely collapsed, but they were not completely wiped out—there are more than 6 million Maya people alive today that carry on the traditions of their ancestors, even with the pressures of the modern world. They farm the same lands their ancestors did and travel the same areas they did, but now these areas have been opened up to tourists, thus disrupting their way of life. During the time of the Spanish conquest, the region was Christianized; however, Maya today follow a mixture of Catholicism and the old ways of their ancestors. Many communities still use the ancient Maya calendar and have a Shaman, or day-keeper, who tracks the energy of the days and conducts traditional rituals. Through political strife and invasion of daily lives through tourism and modernization, the Maya are maintaining their identity and culture and increasing in number rather than dwindling.

The Last Ancient Maya

The final time period associated with ancient Maya studies is the Postclassic. It extended from the collapse of the Classic Maya city-states in AD 900 to the arrival of the Spanish in force in 1524. Some scholars designate the last century of the Classic and the first of the Postclassic as the Terminal Classic Period (from 800 to 1000) because radical changes took place during those centuries, leading to the collapse of the cities.

In a decade-long study published in 2017, researchers developed a precise chronology of the patterns that led to the collapse of the ancient Maya. Using 154 radiocarbon dates, which involves determining the age of organic matter samples through the amounts of carbon the matter contains, researchers found that the collapse happened in waves. Their samples were taken from Ceibal and controlled excavations at its ruins, which allowed researchers to trace population size and increases and decreases in construction. Archaeologist Takeshi Inomata, the study's lead researcher, said "It's not just a simple collapse, but there are waves of collapse … First, there are smaller waves, tied to warfare and some political instability, then comes the major collapse, in which many centers got abandoned. Then there was some recovery in some places, then another collapse."[25] While their findings do not completely answer the question of the culture's collapse, the authors are hoping their study provides a base for other scholars to see if there is a similar pattern at other Maya sites.

Civilization during the Classic Period proved impossible to maintain in the difficult physical environment of the southern Yucatán. Scholars believe overpopulation and overuse of natural resources eventually caused the abandonment of Palenque, Tikal, Cobá, and Copán. With the abandonment of Classic Maya cities in the southern lowlands and the migration of large groups of people from those cities, populated areas in the northern Yucatán and the southern highlands gained influence. There is also a lot of evidence of strong political influence from civilizations in central Mexico.

Postclassic cities in the northern Yucatán lowlands, such as Uxmal, Kabáh, Labná, Chichén Itzá and Mayapán, were apparently influenced in art, architecture, and religious practices by the Toltec, a warlike culture that flourished in central Mexico during the 10th to 12th centuries AD. Postclassic Maya cities were smaller, less decorated, and less skillfully constructed than Classic cities. These changes may have been due either to scarcity of food resulting from drought or as the result of political and military influence from the Toltecs. Many Postclassic cities also had defensive walls surrounding the city's center, possibly indicating constant warfare.

By the time the Spanish arrived in the 1520s, the Maya civilization had evolved into something entirely different from the Classic Period. The Maya had migrated away from their stone cities to two regions: the southern highlands of their Preclassic ancestors, and north and east to the coastal areas of the Yucatán. They remained focused on the calendar, worshipped many gods, and used hieroglyphics. They also established extensive sea trade routes around the Gulf of Mexico and into the Caribbean Sea.

Many Maya ruins, such as the Temple of the Warriors in Chichén Itzá, shown here, still remain today.

No Match for the Spanish

The remaining Maya kingdoms offered fierce resistance to Spain, but they were no match for Spanish firepower, nor did they have defenses against Spanish diseases. During the first 10 to 20 years of Spanish occupation, thousands of Maya died from smallpox and other diseases against which they had no natural immunity. Spanish soldiers brought southern kingdoms under their control by 1527 and northern kingdoms by 1546. Maya kingdoms in isolated forests of the central highlands held out against the Spanish until 1697. Destroyed by warfare and disease, the Maya suffered more than the annihilation of much of

their population. They also suffered the permanent loss of their history at the hands of Spanish priests, who ordered their books to be burned and many of their idols to be smashed. They even told the Maya that they could not speak or use their own language.

However, the Maya endured the collapse of their civilization and the destruction of their numbers from disease. They suffered a long, bloody conquest at the hands of the Spanish, refusing to submit to Spanish control until the final Maya community—Tayasal on Lake Petén Itzá in Guatemala—was conquered in 1697. They endured centuries of discrimination, first at the hands of Spanish colonizers and later, at the hands of descendants of those conquerors who moved into their territory and pushed the Maya to the fringes.

Resistance against outside attempts to destroy their culture has kept the Maya strong and has preserved their culture. In 1847, Maya peasants in the Yucatán rebelled against the high taxes and unfair land policies of newly independent Mexico in a conflict called the Caste War. For more than a year, Maya rebels fought with muskets and machetes until they had control of virtually the entire Yucatán Peninsula. Then, in 1848, on the verge of storming Mérida, the region's largest city, they faltered and were driven back into the eastern jungles.

Regrouping, some Maya established an independent nation called Noj Kaj Santa Cruz Xbalam Naj, also called Chan Santa Cruz ("Little Holy Cross"). It extended along the East Coast of the Yucatán, from just north of the Maya ruins of Tulum, south to what is now the border of Belize. Partly because of extensive trade, the British government recognized Noj Kaj Santa Cruz Xbalam Naj as an independent nation. History books generally list 1901 as the date this independent Maya nation was conquered by Mexican troops, but fierce resistance actually continued into the 1940s. Today, descendants of the rebels live in Quintana Roo, Mexico, and call themselves Cruzo'ob Maya. They still resist integration into the Mexican state.

A Culture in Danger

In the 1970s and 1980s, Maya citizens of Guatemala suffered horribly at the hands of a militaristic government that seemed intent on destroying their culture. On May 29, 1978, a unit of the Guatemalan army opened fire on a group of people protesting land policies. Many of them were Maya. More than 100 protesters were killed. Later, the government instituted a resettlement policy aimed at eliminating native culture, all in the name of unifying the nation under one culture and one language. According to Nikolai Grube,

The suppression of the native population in the early 1980s took on the dimensions of genocide. Union members, Catholic activists, and teachers were abducted by death squads and tortured and murdered. Maya demonstrations fell under storms of bullets, the entire male populations of villages were shot and secretly buried in mass graves ... and children were forced into military service. Maya villages disappeared from the maps, and whole tracts of land (such as the Ixil region) were depopulated. Those who had survived and not fled were forcibly resettled into so-called model villages, whose chessboard patterns of streets were watched by soldiers. The statistics convey an impression of the extent of the bloodbath and the human misery of these years, for which the Maya simply use the Spanish term violencia: *150,000 dead, at least*

1 million refugees in their own country, and 400,000 refugees in neighboring countries, the USA, and Europe.[26]

In 1984, due to pressure from the world community, the Guatemalan government stopped its repressive tactics against the Maya. However, smaller efforts continued in Guatemala and neighboring Mexico. Mayan languages were repressed as "dialects." No mention of pre–Spanish conquest history appeared in Guatemalan or Mexican textbooks. In some cases, the achievements of the Classic Maya were attributed to other cultures. The overwhelming influence of modern North American pop culture on the young also has served to further separate today's Maya from their cultural heritage.

Making Their Voices Heard

Today, in both Mexico and Guatemala, the Maya are making their voices heard. In 1994, a guerrilla group named the Zapatista National Liberation Army (Ejército Zapatista de Liberación Nacional, or EZLN) stormed San Cristóbal de las Casas, a large city in central Chiapas, Mexico. The group waged a protest against the Mexican state. While the EZLN remains alive today, they only receive occasional attention in the media, and they tend to keep to themselves, even running their own schools and health clinics.

Currently, the Maya in Guatemala, the nation with the largest Maya population, are not waging war against their government, but they have reason to hope. Elections in December 1995 brought a national government that was less anti-Maya. Under the United Nations, investigations into human rights violations have started, displaced indigenous peoples are being resettled, cultural identity and human rights have been guaranteed, and Mayan languages are again being taught in schools.

Maya communities are now beginning to organize and play more prominent roles in national politics and public policy making. Maya groups in Mexico, Guatemala, and Belize are demanding the return of control over their ancestors' cities from local governments and foreign archaeologists, museums, and universities. Maya publishers are printing books and establishing websites in Mayan languages. Young Maya are exchanging their Spanish names for names of Maya origin.

Maya politicians—mostly women—have been elected to positions in the national government of Guatemala. Maya archaeologists and epigraphers work side by side with scientists from other countries, striving to make the history, language, and culture of their people known to the world. Maya activists are leading the way in a renewed conservation movement—one designed to preserve the natural environment and to protect their cultural heritage by creating national parks around major Late Preclassic and Classic Maya sites.

During her acceptance of the 1992 Nobel Peace Prize, author and indigenous

Members of the Zapatista National Liberation Army are shown here celebrating the International Day of Indigenous Peoples in 2014.

rights activist Rigoberta Menchú Tum summarized the Maya worldview and their cautious optimism for the future:

> We have in our mind the deepest felt demands of the entire human race, when we strive for peaceful co-existence and the preservation of the environment. The struggle we fight purifies and shapes the future.

> Our history is a living history, that has throbbed, withstood and survived many centuries of sacrifice. Now it comes forward again with strength. The seeds, dormant for such a long time, break out today with some uncertainty, although they germinate in a world that is at present characterized by confusion and uncertainty.[27]

Examining Ancient Sites with Virtual Reality

New technologies are becoming essential for learning more about the daily lives of cultures such as the Maya. Archaeology does not just involve going to ancient sites, it also involves collaborating with scientists and engineers, and there is more collaboration now than ever. Archaeologists have relied on geographic information systems for decades. These systems create two-dimensional images of structures using GPS and other data. However, scientists are now using this information with three-dimensional modeling techniques to create new views of lost worlds. This virtual site is created using Light Detection and Ranging (LiDAR) and photogrammetry. LiDAR uses lasers to calculate distance by measuring the time it takes for the laser pulse to return to the LiDAR device. This system allows scientists to map out the topography of a site. Photogrammetry fills in the details by turning two-dimensional photographs into three-dimensions, thus allowing scholars to create detailed, high resolution models. In 2017, a computer simulation of Copán was created which allowed scholars to walk through the site with a virtual reality system and see what the Maya would have seen. This allows archaeologists to examine sites in a new way, allowing them to ask different questions and understand the lives of these ancient peoples. Even thousands of years after the Maya created their magnificent structures, there is still much to be learned about their daily lives, and scholars are continuing to use the most advanced technology to learn all they can about their remarkably advanced culture.

Notes

Chapter One:
The Maya Rise to Power

1. Nikolai Grube, ed., *Maya: Divine Kings of the Rain Forest*. Nordrhein-Westfalen, DE: h.f. ullmann, 2007, p. 11.

2. Victor Wolfgang von Hagen, *Maya Explorer: John Lloyd Stephens and the Lost Cities of Central America and Yucatán*. Norman, OK: University of Oklahoma Press, 1948, p. 75.

3. Quoted in Bruce Norman, *Footsteps: Nine Archaeological Journeys of Romance and Discovery*. Topsfield, MA: Salem House, 1988, pp. 170–171.

4. Quoted in Norman, *Footsteps*, p. 178.

5. Arthur Demarest, *Ancient Maya: The Rise and Fall of a Rainforest Civilization*. New York, NY: Cambridge University Press, 2004, p. 114.

6. Guy Gugliotta, "The Maya: Glory and Ruin," *National Geographic*, August 2007. ngm.nationalgeographic.com/static-legacy/ngm/0708/feature2/index.html.

Chapter Two:
Noble Maya People

7. Simon Martin and Nikolai Grube, *Chronicle of the Maya Kings and Queens: Deciphering the Dynasties of the Ancient Maya*. London, UK: Thames & Hudson, 2000, p. 14.

8. Nikolai Grube and Simon Martin, "The Dynastic History of the Maya," in *Maya: Divine Kings of the Rain Forest*. Nordrhein-Westfalen, DE: h.f. ullmann, 2007, p. 157.

9. Michael D. Coe, *The Maya*. New York, NY: Thames & Hudson, 2005, p. 207.

10. Coe, *The Maya*, p. 207.

11. Charles Gallenkamp, *Maya: The Riddle and Rediscovery of a Lost Civilization*. New York, NY: Viking Penguin, 1985, p. 126.

Chapter Three:
Common Maya People

12. Demarest, *Ancient Maya*, p. 116.

13. Quoted in Roger Atwood, "Maya Root: Did an Ugly, Waxy Tuber Feed a Great Civilization?" *Archaeology*, July/August 2009, p. 60.

14. Peter D. Harrison, "Maya Agriculture," in *Maya: Divine Kings of the Rain Forest*. Nordrhein-Westfalen, DE: h.f. ullmann, 2007, p. 74.

Chapter Four:
Maya Legacy

15. Heather McKillop, *The Ancient Maya: New Perspectives*. New York, NY: Norton, 2004, p. 293.

16. Michael D. Coe, *Breaking the Maya Code*. New York, NY: Thames & Hudson, 1999, p. 7.

17. Quoted in *NOVA*, "Cracking the Maya Code," PBS, April 8, 2008. www.pbs. org/wgbh/nova/ancient/cracking-maya-code.html.

18. Quoted in *NOVA*, "Cracking the Maya Code."

19. Quoted in Grube, ed., *Maya*, p. 143.

20. Quoted in Grube, ed., *Maya*, p. 141.

Chapter Five:
Spirits and the Universe

21. Quoted in Grube, ed., *Maya*, p. 268.

22. McKillop, *The Ancient Maya*, p. 218.

23. Quoted in Grube, ed., *Maya*, p. 265.

24. Demarest, *Ancient Maya*, p. 192.

Epilogue:
The Maya Today

25. Quoted in Sarah Pruitt, "What Caused the Maya Collapse? Archaeologists Uncover New Clues," The History Channel, January 25, 2017. www.history.com/news/what-caused-the-maya-collapse-archaeologists-uncover-new-clues.

26. Grube, ed., *Maya*, p. 422.

27. Rigoberta Menchú Tum, "Rigoberta Menchú Tum Nobel Lecture," NobelPrize.org, December 10, 1992. www.nobelprize.org/nobel_prizes/peace/laureates/1992/tum-lecture.html.

For More Information

Books

Banquedano, Elizabeth, and Clark, Barry. *Aztec, Inca, and Maya*. New York, NY: DK, 2005.

    Stunning photos, full-color art, and informative text give an overview of these three pre-Columbian civilizations.

Carlson, William. *Jungle of Stone: The Extraordinary Journey of John L. Stephens and Frederick Catherwood, and the Discovery of the Lost Civilization of the Maya*. New York, NY: William Morrow, 2017.

    This thrilling book thoroughly examines the Maya as well as the adventures and discoveries of John Lloyd Stephens and Frederick Catherwood.

Coe, Michael D. *The Maya*. New York, NY: Thames & Hudson, 2005.

    This complete study of the Maya was written by a leading Maya scholar and includes plenty of photographs.

Frimmer, Steven. *The Man Who Found the Maya*. Bloomington, IN: Xlibris, 2010.

    This book tells the story of explorer John Lloyd Stephens and his incredible discoveries about the Maya people.

Phillips, Charles. *The Illustrated Encyclopedia of Aztec and Maya: The History, Legend, Myth and Culture of the Ancient Native Peoples of Mexico and Central America*. London, UK: Southwater Publishing, 2017.

    This book gives newly updated information about the Aztec, Maya, Toltec, and Olmec people, and it includes images of artifacts and fascinating archaeological sites.

Websites

"In Search of the Lost Empire of the Maya"
(www.nationalgeographic.com/magazine/2016/09/maya-empire-snake-kings-dynasty-mesoamerica/)
　　This article provides information on the Snake Kings of the Maya culture and provides aerial video of the stunning archaeological site.

Joya de Cerén Archaeological Site
(whc.unesco.org/en/list/675)
　　This United Nations World Heritage website includes interesting photos and plenty of information on the fascinating archaeological finds of Cerén.

Maya: Facts and Summary
(www.history.com/topics/maya)
　　This website has a wealth of information on the Maya, including videos, facts, and a timeline.

NG Live!: Palenque and the Ancient Maya World
(video.nationalgeographic.com/video/ng-live/stuarts-lecture-nglive)
　　This National Geographic documentary provides information about and stunning footage of the Palenque site.

"These Technologies are Giving New Life to the Ancient World"
(www.nbcnews.com/mach/science/these-technologies-are-giving-new-life-ancient-world-ncna792921)
　　This article provides information on how the newest technologies are helping archaeologists piece together information on ancient cultures.

Index

Tum, Rigoberta Menchú, 7, 93

U
United Nations, 57, 92
Uxmal, 13, 16, 62, 89
uytzam chinamital, 36

V
Venus, 63, 72, 80
virtual reality, 94
volcano, 14, 45
Voss, Alexander W., 69, 72

W
World Tree, 77–78, 82
Wuqub' Junajpu, 79–80

X
Xb'alanke, 79–80
Xibalba, 73–74, 76, 79–80, 82–83, 85

Y
yalba uinicob, 31, 42
Yucatán, 7, 15–16, 24, 35, 40, 48, 51, 58,
   62, 66, 76, 86, 89, 91
Yum Cimil, 85

Z
Zapatista National Liberation Army
   (Ejército Zapatista de Liberación
   Nacional, or EZLN), 92–93
zero, 68

Picture Credits

Cover DEA/G. DAGLI ORTI/De Agostini/Getty Images; pp. 6–7 (background) JoseIgnacioSoto/iStock/Thinkstock; p. 6 (left) Atypeek/iStock/Thinkstock; p. 6 (top-right) Jose CABEZAS/AFP/Getty Images; p. 6 (bottom-right) DEA/ G. DAGLI ORTI/Contributor/Getty Images; pp. 7 (top), 20–21, 25, 41, 56, 57, 74–75, 86, 90 DeAgostini/Getty Images; p. 7 (bottom-left) mbrand85/ Shutterstock.com; p. 7 (bottom-right) MIGUEL ROJO/AFP/Getty Images; pp. 10–11 soft_light/Shutterstock.com; pp. 13, 45, 46–47 Matyas Rehak/ Shutterstock.com; pp. 14–15 El Comandante/Wikimedia Commons; p. 18 Science History Images/Alamy Stock Photo; pp. 26–27 DR Travel Photo and Video/Shutterstock.com; p. 30 Richard Maschmeyer/robertharding/Getty Images; p. 32 De Agostini/Archivio J. Lange/Getty Images; p. 35 BERTRAND GUAY/AFP/Getty Images; p. 38 Terry W. Rutledge/National Geographic/ Getty Images; p. 39 MARTIN BUREAU/AFP/Getty Images; p. 43 Roy H. Anderson/National Geographic/Getty Images; p. 49 3000RISK/iStock/ Thinkstock; pp. 52, 84 Werner Forman/Universal Images Group/Getty Images; pp. 54–55 JOHAN ORDONEZ/AFP/Getty Images; p. 59 Niciak/iStock/ Thinkstock; pp. 60–61 Wolfgang Kaehler/Contributor/LightRocket/Getty Images; pp. 64–65 SL-Photography/Shutterstock.com; pp. 66–67 milosk50/ Shutterstock.com; p. 69 Gordiienko Tetiana/Shutterstock.com; p. 70 Stefano Ember/Shutterstock.com; p. 71 Ralf Broskvar/Shutterstock.com; pp. 76–77 javarman/Shutterstock.com; pp. 78–79 Jos+1⁄4 M. Osorio/Chicago Tribune/MCT via Getty Images; pp. 80–81 PHAS/UIG via Getty Images; p. 93 ELIZABETH RUIZ/AFP/Getty Images.

About the Author

Emily Mahoney is the author and editor of over a dozen nonfiction books for young readers on various topics. She has a Master's Degree in Literacy from the University at Buffalo and a Bachelor's Degree from Canisius College in Adolescent Education and English. She currently teaches reading to middle school students and loves watching her students learn how to become better readers and writers. She enjoys reading, Pilates, yoga, and spending time with family and friends. She lives with her husband in Buffalo, New York, where she was born and raised.